Virtue Rewarded

George and Addey

Virtue Rewarded

LOVE LETTERS OF

GEORGE VIRTUE & ADDEY WATSON

1848–1855

Edited and with commentary by

Diane Sargent

their great-granddaughter

ISBN 978-0-692-14778-8

Printed in Portland, Maine, by Walch Education and Printing

Book design by Ruth Maassen

Front cover photograph by Lee Nadel

For Yhanna,
with thanks,
Deedee

Dedication

To those responsible for

securing safe passage of the letters

to their direct descendants~

Harriet Louisa Virtue,

Mary Fillingham,

and my sister Joyce

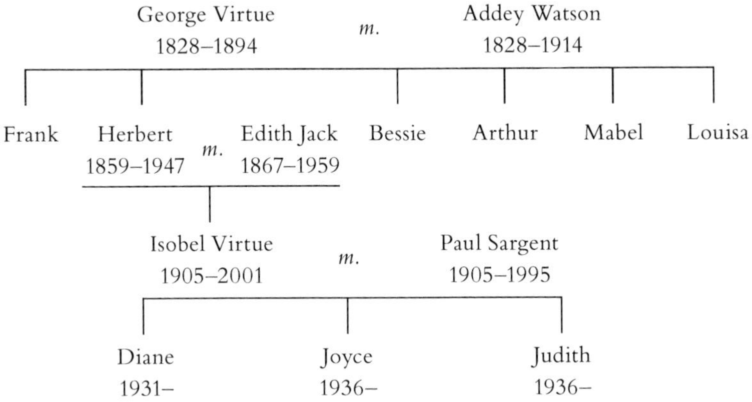
George Virtue
1828–1894
m.
Addey Watson
1828–1914
Frank
Herbert
1859–1947
m.
Edith Jack
1867–1959
Bessie
Arthur
Mabel
Louisa
Isobel Virtue
1905–2001
m.
Paul Sargent
1905–1995
Diane
1931–
Joyce
1936–
Judith
1936–

Contents

Introduction

One never knows when the past will make its way into the present.

Virtue was my mother's maiden name: Isobel Macpherson Virtue. It was also the name of the small family publishing firm established in London in 1813 by George Virtue. His nephew, also named George Virtue, was my mother's grandfather. The name of the firm, Virtue & Company, Limited, evoked smiles from those of my friends who wrote me when I used it as a forwarding address while traveling in Europe many years ago.

The surname Virtue was originally the French *Vertu*. Huguenots by that name emigrated to Scotland during the late sixteenth century to escape religious persecution. Some eventually made their way south to England, where the name was anglicized to Virtue.

During the early 1970s, an English cousin of my mother's, Mary Fillingham, discovered a cache of 122 letters in a house she had inherited in Topsham, in the south of England. They were written during the mid-nineteenth century by my mother's grandparents, George Virtue and Adelaide Watson, during their courtship. Mary felt they should come to us, their direct descendants.

Soon afterward, my sister Joyce picked them up. All were carefully folded, most in their original envelopes, and packed neatly into a painted Victorian candy box. Some dried flowers were still pressed between the tissue-thin pages.

The writing was as finely wrought as Chinese calligraphy and almost as incomprehensible. Joyce described Addey's handwriting as looking like a fine thread ripped from a hem and dropped onto a piece of paper. Many were cross-hatched in the custom of the day, whereby to save paper, each side is written on twice, the second time at right angles to the first, making an "8 sider."

With no small measure of time, energy, patience, and perseverance, Joyce was able to transcribe them. I have selected excerpts from the letters and added commentary.

That the letters, for all their age and fragility, have survived well over 170 years is remarkable enough, but their falling into the hands of the direct descendants of those who wrote them seems nothing short of a miracle. The voices of George and Addey cross the deep abyss of time, revealing an endearing pair of young lovers, inhabitants of a world long vanished, who express their hopes and fears, their joy and despair as they struggle toward a happy outcome to their courtship.

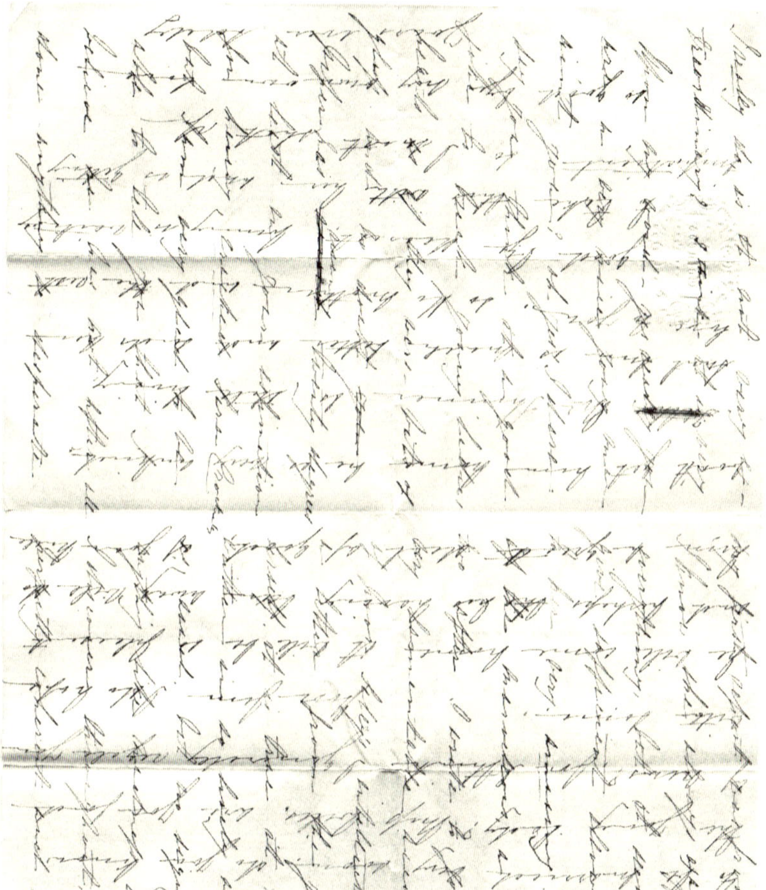

A cross-hatched page from one of Addey's letters to George.

List of Illustrations

PART I

George in Devon

1848

Only a little bit of jasamine!!

And so their story begins. In January of 1848, George Virtue and Adelaide Watson meet at a winter ball. Both are 19.

Addey lives in Devon, near the southwest coast of England, with her father, mother, and two sisters, Alicia and Winnie, both of whom are engaged to be married. Their home is Bowdon Lodge, a small gabled stone house a short distance outside of Totnes.

The Watsons live comfortably. Evidently they had been landed gentry before Addey's grandfather, Humphrey Watson, gambled away the family inheritance. And yet there is no suggestion of deprivation or hardship in the letters. Addey and George are obviously well-educated. Thomas, Addey's father, is a nursery gardener.

George is from Bristol and still has family there. He has recently taken a job as assistant station agent with the recently established South Devon Railway.

George and Addey see each other often in the early days. They have no need to write letters until May, when George is transferred to the railroad station at Newton Abbot a few miles away, and they can spend time together only on the weekends. And with this first separation, the letters begin.

18 May 1848

[Addey to George]

Just as I was going to put on my bonnet with the intention of walking in to the town to find out if there was any letter from you, little Richard Taylor brought me one which I was well pleased to receive, short though it be, but with the hope of having a long one next time you write. I am contented with this, the more so when I see by the date you wrote it on Tuesday.

I do miss you so much evenings. They pass so quietly and so lonelily with nothing but reading and thinking about you, and really it seems to me that the latter employment is the more pleasant, somehow. I wish you were in Totnes now but I shall see you again on Sunday, dearest, only two days more after this evening! I wonder if the anticipation affords you as much pleasure as it does me?

I shall not write any more for I heard you say you disliked reading writing that is crossed, so for fear of making *you* cross I will say goodbye and I wish you a pleasant promenade.

Your little Addey

Friday morn

[Addey to George]

Yes, my own darling, I have answered you, but what did you think, what could you have thought – to have written to me like this? You thought I intentionally deferred writing you?

But, dearest, I did not think you would have written until Wednesday when I thought I should have it yesterday, or I would have gone in before, and last evening there was brought this very concise note, and you cannot think how I was hurt by it. But you are not angry now, are you, love? And rest assured, I shall always answer your letters as soon as received.

Father is now going so I have no more time, only to beg of you not to fail coming on Sunday.

Yours ever,
Addey

These early missives are laced with teasing and tenderness, revealing George and Addey's growing affection for one another, as well as relating the happenings of their daily lives, along with an occasional misunderstanding when letters did not arrive at the expected time.

May 24, 1848

[Addey to George]

What a lovely morning! I am just returned from a most delightful walk and have been trying to discover the place of your abode. But I am afraid I have failed although I have settled on a pretty place on the side of a hill by Newton, which I fancy may be the very spot. At least I wish it may be for I can see it plainly, and then with a slight stretch of imagination you know I can even fancy I can see you there also. Altho' very improbable it is nevertheless pleasant to think so.

I am much obliged for the "Model Wife." I think it excellent. I shall certainly not part with it for I fancy I may require it as much as anybody else, altho' you were kind enough to say I should not. There is one fault of which I should not be guilty for certain and that is appearing at the breakfast table in "curl papers," and as to "flirting," which you took the trouble to underline, it is a pasttime to which I am not at all addicted, and if ever I have the misfortune (& I have no doubt it would be a very big one) to get a husband I am very much afraid he would not find in me a "Model Wife." Now after that confession I hope you will be candid enough to own that I am not "conceited," but I don't suppose you will either.

I think I ought to be indulged in a *long* letter sometimes, say next time? For you know you are going away, dear, and I shall not have you here to talk to, and so you must let me have a nice long letter before you go away that I may have something to read from you on Sunday. Now you will gratify me this once, won't you? Yes! There's a darling!

I wish you were in Totnes now, for it used to be such pleasure to look forward to the evening in expectation of seeing you, and then as the time of your coming would be passing, there would be the hope that you would come, and the fear that you would not. All this is passed and I suppose I ought not to have said anything about it. By some I know I should be condemned for allowing you to know that I care so much about you. Am I wrong? No, I think not, for you knew it all before.

29 June 1848 Bowdon

[Addey to George]

I went in to the town yesterday but not until the evening, so I received your *two* epistles just together. In fact, I read the last you sent first. I was afraid something was the matter, so I broke it open in trembling haste, regardless of the rules of etiquette, but when I found there was no need for alarm, I became quite happy. And so you were pleased with my last letter? I am glad of it. Although do you know I almost wished after I had sent it that I could again get it in my possession. I don't quite know why. I didn't think you would be angry, but then I was half inclined to think you would fancy I need not have said so much, but if you had no such thought, love, I am not at all sorry I sent it.

And I have picked another rose bud for you, which I hope will atone for my not sending one the other day after promising – it is a *better* one though not perhaps quite so *pretty*, inasmuch as it is *thornless* for it would ill beseem me to send you *thorns. It should rather be my office to extract them.*

I was half afraid you would be left behind – and I almost expected to hear – your – long whistle (sweet sound!) next morning. I went to the door two or three times to listen, but now all was silent as the wind and the birds would allow it to be. And allow me to convince you of my unselfishness when I tell you I was *not sorry* I did not hear it, or see you, for I knew, at least thought, that you would rather have been in time than otherwise.

Mother has just been in. "What – writing again, Addey?" Yes, my "gentle Geordie," and I would like to be always writing to you when I am not talking or listening to you or reading your kind letters. And this puts me in mind that I ought to thank you for yours of yesterday and I do, my dear, dear Virtue, most heartily.

I have sometimes doubted and pondered within myself whether you *really* do love me or not and then perhaps a word or look may rise to my remembrance which leaves me still doubting, but this is not often, for generally my conclusion is "Yes, bless him, he does love me!" Indeed, how can I doubt what you say. No, I never will, and I do not. Virtue, I *must* believe you for I cannot look at your face (would I could now) so full of truth and frank sincerity and disbelieve anything you say (when you are speaking in earnest). No, I place full and entire confidence in you and I know you deserve it.

By your saying Mr. Clarke is "all right" I presume you mean that he has *not* resigned. If such be the case I am very glad of it, for your sake, as it will prevent his going for a soldier and also your remaining at home after his departure, "but my heart will be with you wherever you may go." But still I hope you won't go farther away. Oh! the selfishness of human nature! But I won't begin to moralize, but say good bye to you at once and I will go as far as the top of the hill but I mustn't go out of sight.

Yours,
Addey

1 July 1848

South Devon Railway
Newton Station

My dear Addey,

Of course you expect me to write today, don't you? & if your feelings in this respect, are at all similar to mine, I know well what a disappointment you will feel at not receiving one after expecting it, & therefore I must come up with something for you to read this evening – I think you are a very good little prophetess. It is a beautiful morning & likely to remain fine all day. I hope it will continue so tomorrow – I dislike rainy weather so *much*.

And you wanted to keep your last letter, did you? Oh! What a loss it would have been to me if you had persisted in doing so. I think it *possible that I love you more and more* every day, & I feel so happy to think you love me also – & yet I can hardly believe that you really & truly love me, but time will tell, Addey dearest. One thing is certain, I can *never* love anyone but you. I do not mean to say that you have ever given me cause to doubt your regard for me – far from it – Addey. I think you are the only girl who ever had any real sort of love for me – & I feel so proud to think I possess yours – but I cannot help fearing that it will change. I hope not & I trust it never will – but I am getting myself into such a true lover's knot – I'm afraid if I don't leave off at once I shall not be able to extricate myself at all. If true love consists of making fine speeches & all that sort of thing, I shall fall very short.

Do you know, Addey, when I got home the other night I thought over my conduct to you in the evening so much so that I could not sleep for a long time. I fancy I know how you felt when I turned away from you as you tripped over to me and looked at me. Oh 'twas very unkind of me, indeed. I felt I had acted harshly the moment afterwards – & what I blamed myself most for was because I did not outwardly return & beg your pardon. But I do now, Addey, with all my heart and you will not refuse me, I know. You are too kind-hearted for that.

I am rather busy today so excuse me if I leave off now. I will not promise again but will *endeavor* without doing so to come over to-morrow per 5:40.

George, I am quite smitten. Your questioning of your behavior to Addey is touching.

Bowdon Lodge

A few years ago, I was able to visit the small stone house where Addey lived, with its casement windows and steeply pitched roof. An elderly widow, Dorothy Trigg, greeted me when I knocked at the front door. She welcomed me warmly and invited me in. She was eager to learn about George and Addey, and the letters. We sipped cups of strong English tea as we chatted about my research.

Seeing the comfortable house still standing made me realize how brave Addey had been to leave it for an uncertain life on the other side of the Atlantic with George.

5 July 1848

South Devon Railway
Newton Station

My dear Addey,

Oh my! How you have frightened me! & how very sorry I am I could not get down to the lower station to see you off. I don't know when Mr. Clarke has been more busy than he was this evening (it always happens so). When I first came back from tea, he was knee deep in business. He said then that I should not be able to assist in the Booking Office at all & that they might manage without Mr. Hannaford the best way they could, but in a quarter of an hour I put all to rights for the time being & then rushed down to the lower station & staid there ("on thorns nearly") till within a minute of your starting time & then I was obliged to go up to my own office again & leave you to your fate. I told the porter to look out for you & open the doors again if you should come. However, I'm very glad you were in time after all, for I should have been very uneasy if you had been left behind & I'm sure you would have been the same. You must come over some day when Mr. Clarke is out of the way & be here longer & I'll try then if I cannot make you more comfortable.

And you thought I should be very ill last Sunday, did you? You are wrong for once, my little son! or nearly so, but I forgot to tell you I was down at the station (Totnes) in very good time (11 p.m.) & had to wait there about half an hour.

When I got home last night, good old Dick was gone to bed very ill, & he was no better this morning when I left him. I think it is a sort of ague he has. I fancied I was rather poorly & went home early in the evening on purpose but when I saw poor Dick, he cured me directly. I had a slight relapse this morning, perhaps by being disturbed at about 2 a.m. by Long Tom Arly & Tom Bastin. They were out on a sort of a spree & wanted me to dress & come down into Newton with them. I very modestly declined, strongly advising them at the same time, if they had any respect for their precious health they would be far better home in bed & not be disturbing honest folks at that time of night (or morning). After about 20 minutes parley, I at last got rid of them but I could not sleep much after they left & I have caught a cold in consequence which makes me feel rather queer. But it's a beautiful morning and as the "little man" is up, I shall take the advantage of a nice walk which I hope will be the means of making me all right. At all events, I shall be well by tomorrow (I hope).

Here I am again! Hannaford & I have just returned from rather a long but certainly a most beautiful walk. We have been to Kingsteignton village. I feel very much better for my walk but very warm – & now, little Addey, am I not a selfish individual to keep so continually talking about the first person singular and not asking you a word as to how you are after your trip? – How you enjoyed yourself (but I'm sure you did not enjoy yourself much as it was a very *unpropitious* day for you to come). Next time you must come over by an early train & pay Highweek a visit –

May I expect to hear from you before Sunday? If you get this letter in anything like reasonable time, I know you will! Won't you?

I'll not say anything about coming over on Sunday yet. You may expect to hear from me Saturday evening.

Addey I *do not doubt* your affection!!! What I meant by saying I wish I could come over often was because I think you must be very lonely at Bowdon by yourself. *And* I should like you to have a fitter companion than Lizzy Taylor.

Yours ever,
George

Highweek is the section of Newton Abbot where George lived with the Drew family.

7 JULY 1848 BOWDON

[Addey to George]

I have just obtained possession of your letter, and I thank you for it. I could not go in for it yesterday although I expected there was one waiting for me, but I have it now.

It was such a wonder that we had not been left behind on Wednesday. We had to run so fast, and then were but just in time. The train was off before we could get in. I nearly fell back on the platform, if the porter had not by his hand prevented such a scene. I enquired for you and the man said you were "up with Mr. Clarke" and "couldn't get away." I was very much disappointed, yet very glad that we were in time. Oh! If we had been left behind!

You are mistaken in imagining I did not enjoy myself, for I did, though of course not as much as if you had had more time to be with us. I like Mrs. Drew and her pretty daughter-in-law very much.

Thank you, dear, for the reason you have given for wishing to be home oftener. You really do think you would be a "fitter companion" for me than Lizzie Taylor? Well, I am not going to say you are not, but she is *not often* a companion of mine. I will confess freely that I do not like her well enough to be with her oftener than I can help. I want not company. You are enough for me, and when you are not here, (which is generally), I have your letters at a look and last though not least, my own thoughts. I will not tell you on what they love to linger, but they are not often of a sombre cast, and I am generally happy. Do not say you are selfish when you write to me of yourself.

Anything that concerns you must always have more interest for me than anything else can have. Write and talk to me then of yourself. Are you better than you were when you wrote to me?

So you don't know about coming on Sunday? Yes, do! But you will tell me tomorrow, won't you? I hope you will, but you know that, don't you, and if you are not *particularly engaged,* you will come, I know.

What do you think I have just been amusing myself about? You will never guess so to put an end at once to your curiosity, I will tell you. I have just taken the trouble then to count the number of *words* in your letter! And how many do you think there are? Why, 816! But there will be more in mine when I have finished, and to save you the trouble, or to gratify my own present humour, I will count them myself, also.

I can't go out for 'tis raining, oh the everlasting rain!

Oh, by the way, I had almost forgotten to tell you that I have been invited to go to Dartmouth with a party who are going next week when Phil comes down. "Who is Phil?" Well, I will tell you. He is a cousin of the Taylor's who, of course, will be of the party, and I know, dearest, you will not be displeased when I tell you that I have positively declined going. Was that right? I should not enjoy myself if I were to go.

I hope I may be able to get this to the post today or you will not have it till tomorrow evening. Well, what must be, will be, and if it does rain and my mother will not allow me to go with this myself to the office, you know I cannot control necessity and you must wait 'till tomorrow evening before you can hear from

Your little Addey

I told Mother yesterday that I had been to Newton. She was not at all angry.

I knew I would have more words than you.

8 July 1848 Newton Station

Dear Addey,

Just this moment read your letter, & just having about 3 minutes to spare, I'll send you this scrawl just to keep you in a good temper. I will not promise you I'll come tomorrow as I think it likely Mr. Clarke will want me – if he should not, I'll try & come over per 6:40, but *do you go to Dartmouth,* there's a little dear. I'll write more fully tomorrow if I do not come over.

Train just in – this is only an apology for a note! So don't attempt to count the words. If I don't come tomorrow you shall have a regular 8 sider & no mistake.

Let me go;
God bless you,
Ever yours
George

I am writing this in the Booking Office, & am continually being pestered by passengers asking for tickets.

➢ *Isn't it your job to sell tickets, George? (Not that that means you can't complain.) And good for you to urge Addey to go on that trip to Dartmouth.*

Mail Service

No residential delivery existed then. Letters were taken to an office, often in a small shop, to be sent on to another similar destination where they would be picked up. Originally the postage was paid by the recipient. There were no stamps at first, nor envelopes. The Penny Post, established in the 1850s, used the new railway system to deliver to different parts of the country. As the letters often indicate, delivery was surprisingly quick, better than today.

15 July 1848

South Devon Railway
Newton

My dear Addey,

Here! I have but a very short time to spare this morning, as I want to finish my work up close that I may have nothing to do tomorrow (pious resolution!!). Mr. Gedge has kindly invited both of us to spend the day (or *a portion of it*) with him tomorrow at Joy Bridge. Presuming you will not object to the trip I have taken upon myself to give your consent – as well as my own. Now, you will go, Addey, won't you? I have also taken upon myself to arrange this matter; *viz.* to start from Totnes, pr 1:30 p.m. Are you agreeable, Miss? *Very well* then. Now, let me see, if I can manage it (& I think I can) I will run down to Totnes tonight, arriving there about 10:30 pm (London time). If you have not shut up shop I may perhaps be in time to see you home, but don't you wait for me later than 10:30, there's a little dear. In fact, I don't wish you to wait at all for me (& I hope you will not do so!) as

I shall see you the first thing tomorrow morning. I intend coming up to Bowdon to breakfast, & then if you would rather go to Joy Bridge at 8 a.m. instead of at 1:30 p.m. I shall be very happy to go then also.

Now you know, Miss Watson, if it should come to rain tomorrow, *much*, it will of course put a damper upon the whole proceedings (barring my coming over) & am sorry to say that the clouds look very promising for showers at present. If it should be very wet, I'll not come over until Bath Mail [train] & we won't think of going then, but defer it till the next fine Sunday. I think I will venture to say that you *may* venture to expect me sometime between this evening & 1:30 tomorrow. You little puss, I'm quite longing to see you again. Bless your heart. Good bye, dearest. I'll see you tomorrow or perhaps tonight,

G. Virtue

The 7:30 a.m. up this way cut a policeman's head off!!

> ➢ *In an envelope is a scrap of paper with the words "Only a little bit of jasamine!!" and a pressed flower from George to Addey.*
>
> *George, you are not typical of your gender. Usually Victorian ladies sent flowers to their beloveds. How refreshing to see this custom reversed.*

Empty envelope, postmarked 30 July 1848

> ➢ *How I long to know what was once in it. Letters often lose the envelopes they come in, but why would envelopes be kept without their contents?*

28 August 1848

South Devon Railway
Newton

This will be a short one also. I said I would write though – so

My dear Addey,

How are you today? I got down to the station in good time last night & what is still more wonderful, I didn't smash any of the peaches! I got home about 8:30 raining like (nothing) and I gave the fine peach to Mrs. Drew and the others to Lizzy. They both expressed warm thanks, more especially when I told them with what hardihood you tramped through mud & rain to fetch them. Ah! I hope you did not catch cold by doing so. If you have, please to attribute it all to my thoughtlessness in asking you to go out in such weather. You are such a dear little creature. You always try & anticipate my wishes – too kind to me, I'm afraid. I mean to say I don't think I am kind enough to you in return. If I sometimes appear unkind towards you, it is not for want of feeling, Addey, dear. No, really, it is not. I am too thoughtless, but perhaps as I grow older I may grow wiser & then I shall be more attentive; fonder I cannot be. That's some consolation.

Tell Winnie, Alicia's letter went up last night in good time, but I forgot to take away the book she promised to lend me last Friday week. I beg your pardon for not having yet returned you "The Home." I sent it to Bristol a long time ago & Bill has not yet returned it.

Mr. Clarke is gone for the day but he has left plenty for me to do in his absence so excuse this & you shall have a longer one next time. Write soon & believe me

Yours ever,
Geo Virtue

8:30 p.m.

Dear Addey,

Then I haven't had a bit of time before now – all day – Mr. Clarke did not return till late today & consequently all the work's behind hand & I am put off from coming down tomorrow morning as I first intended, but I have no doubt I shall be able to come per 5:45. I should much like to come over to dinner but you see we cannot always have our own way. Well, it's very dark & Dick Drew is standing outside the door whistling & waiting for me to finish.

I suppose you will get this tomorrow church time.

Good day,
Geo Virtue

I'm sorry you will not get this tonight, but it really is not my fault.

The letters reveal George's feelings toward Addey. I have quite lost my heart to him.

Letter Writing

We have been a family of letter writers – and savers of same. My father's mother insisted that her three adult sons write her weekly. I can remember hers to me written on the tissue-thin airmail paper in bright emerald ink. She filled her pages with comments and opinions, sometimes contentious. My father, her youngest, kept carbon copies of his to her so he would have proof of what he had said.

I hope personal letter writing does not vanish into the vortex of electronic communication – a poor substitute, as far as I'm concerned.

[UNDATED]
TUESDAY EVENING

[Addey to George]

"You are a nice one"! Oh – yes, you know how to make me laugh when I would be angry but you have given me full and free permission to "blow you up" – and I think I will, so I beg you will look very serious and – never – presume to smile and so for an excuse for not coming over, you have told me about your intended excursion to Hayton Rock where you did *not* go, yet as this you say "ended in smoke" while it was yet *morning*, I can still discover no reason for your not coming in the *evening*, unless indeed you were so entirely overcome with disappointment at the failure of your project as to feel no inclination to bestir yourself for the remainder of the day! Was this the case? If so, I most freely forgive you. I wish you had gone though since you didn't come here, because I think you would have enjoyed it.

I hope you won't be so unkind as not to come next Sunday, will you? for I shall be *all alone* if you don't, but you will come, won't you, dearest? I am glad that the length of my last pleased you. I like to know that you are pleased with me. I am afraid this will not be so long; I went in this afternoon fully determined that if there was no letter from you, I would not write (although I thought you would expect to hear from me) until I had heard. And I wished I had kept it, too! Do you know that when I found there was no communication from you yesterday, I thought you were angry with me for something or other – what I knew not – or I don't know hardly what I thought, but I am glad nevertheless that all my fears have proved groundless, for I *did* expect you though I tried to persuade myself all the day that I did *not*.

Wednesday morning. I wish you could see me now. I have just been making bread and biscuits. By the way, you shall have some of my manufacture on Sunday when you come over. My sleeves are turned back and my hands have a few grains of flour about them. In fact, I look quite a person of business, but what do you care how I look? Well, I can't help it. I have to let you know I am in a wonderfully good temper. I should like a hearty laugh just now. I have just been indulging in one about *yourself*, now don't frown. It was at your dialogue with Mr. Drew and the picture which you presented to my mind's eye as you sleepily asked him what he wanted.

There Winnie is come down dressed to go in to town so I will with your permission finish at once that she may take this with her. Oh dear! I shall be a most forlorn maiden by and by when she is gone. I wish you were still in Totnes! but there! I have so often wished it that it has become quite useless to wish it any longer, so I won't – if I can help it.

Well, this is the last side, and I *must* finish now whether I will or no. But I could write as much more for I am in a gossiping humour. However, as Winnie is bothering me to make haste, I suppose I must. Goodbye, dearest, write to me again this week, won't you? Winnie's love, together with that of all the rest, dog included – he expressed his loving intention by the wagging of his tail – and amongst all the inclusions, don't forget

Your little Addey

4 September 1848 Newton Abbot

My dear Sweetheart,

How are you this morning? Quite well, I hope. Is not this fine, healthy weather. It's a sin for anyone to lie ill such a day as this. We have just had the Mayor & Corporation of Crabtree here to pay us a visit. They are gone on in a special train to Exeter. They have a fine band of music & all appear very happy.

What did you do all yesterday? It was a shame of me not to come down, for I think I could have done so if I had tried. In fact, I made up my mind to do so in the evening, but as usual, thought of it just in time to be too late. Dear Addey, you will pardon me, won't you now? I assure you I felt very miserable all the evening, & I daresay you expected me over, too – did you? But I will come over next Sunday & stay all day, that is if you do not lecture me & send me away again. You are too good-tempered for that though, you little darling.

I had a ride to Torquay Friday as I believe I told you I should. The young ladies were all very well, but I had not time to stay there a minute scarcely so I did not see much of them. Miss Glanville is still there. I like Miss Glanville, I think a very nice, quiet, good girl!

I don't call this a regular one, you know, so you must excuse its brevity. I hope I shall receive a letter from you today for I fully expect one & you do not often disappoint me. So good morning,

Yours sincerely,
Geo. Virtue

You & Winnie go & take a walk to Bowdon immediately. I am quite ashamed of you both, staying in the house such a healthy morning as this is – go along, Miss –

Love to all

9 September 1848

South Devon Railway
Newton Abbot

Dear Addey,

I find I shall not be able to come by the first train tomorrow but you may expect me by Bath Mail. I will try hard to come then. I have been hard at it all day & I shall not have finished till late tonight.

I could not write per 5:45 & I shall entrust this to the care of Drew so if you don't get it tonight it won't be my fault.

Much in haste,
George

Fragment of a letter of Addey's:

We entered an old house, once the palace of Charles the Second. It really was the most interesting thing we saw during the day, the black oak paneling and the national arms over the fireplace, and the seraphs' heads in the ceiling. The collections of birds and insects were beautiful. The present proprietor thereof is a bachelor, and what do you think, we actually went up in his bedroom! – to see the painted canvas with which the walls were covered. I should so like you to see it. It is very old indeed, and the perspective is most ridiculous. There is a peacock perched upon a tree about half its size. All the contents of the house are great curiosities, the bachelor included, for he is a strange-looking old man with such a cracked voice and he squints. The staircase was perfectly dark. After we had seen and admired all we saw in the palace, our gentlemen were compelled to leave us, but before doing so they left us in the charge of Mr. Crawford (an entire stranger to all but Annie) who very kindly took us out round the castle in a boat. Oh! It was delightful, such a charming swell in the water. And we rode over the waves gallantly, came back to Dartmouth to tea, which we were obliged to hurry over to be in time for the Steamer, and returned to Totnes very much pleased with our excursion. What a lovely river ours is! Have you been down it? There! I think you ought to be very much obliged to me for giving you such a minute description of our pleasant trip to Dartmouth!

23 September 1848 Newton Abbot

My dear Addey,

I have just received a letter from Bill written by him yesterday evening & he actually says he *really* is coming down tonight. I should hardly think he will disappoint me this time. At all events, I shall put faith enough in what he says to go as far as Exeter this evening to meet him.

I received your letter with much pleasure.

You have been to Dartmouth then, have you? I am much pleased to learn you enjoyed yourselves so. I fancy I see you going up the *dark* staircase to the old bachelor's bedroom, but if 'twas dark, I couldn't see you. It was a very mysterious staircase though, I have no doubt, & I suppose the Misses Crockwell & company took great care that you were not frightened. They should have done so at all events. Dark staircases are dangerous places, I know from experience.

Brother Bill must just wait till the wet weather comes in so that it may dampen his courage I suppose. I hope it will clear off though. Do you think it will be fine tomorrow? There is not much appearance of it at present. Wet or dry, I shall come over tomorrow (provided always that I get leave from the Skipper) & if Bill comes down tonight, well & good, I will bring him down with me. As I shall see you tomorrow, then let me go now, Addey, like a darling.

Love to Winnie & co & believe me,
Yours affectionately,
Geo. Virtue

Try to persuade Miss Glanville of the absurdity of her thinking of going home yet – quite preposterous! – can't listen to it a moment. Oh no!

➣ *That remark about the dark staircase sounds ominous.*

Empty envelope from George to Addey, postmarked 5 October 1848

The River Dart in Totnes

My Trip to Dartmouth

When I was in Totnes, I took the same voyage down the River Dart on a small river boat. It was a relaxed and meandering journey. Modest fishing boats were anchored here and there on the calm and shallow water. Boughs of giant oaks overhanging the banks made reflections and provided a leafy fringe as they cast their shadows. The captain of our vessel told us that Dart was the old Celtic word for oak.

On the verdant hills beyond were houses, some rather grand like one which belonged to Agatha Christie, and others as appealing, but more modest. It was an idyllic scene and one I thought may have changed little from when Addey was there.

When we arrived at Dartmouth, a busy port filled with marine activity greeted us. At the entrance to the harbor was a large dry dock, a concrete basin with boats tipping every which way, having no water to support them. When we disembarked, I explored some of the back streets. Many of the houses had flowers cascading from second-floor window boxes to the street below, with prodigious blooms in vivid hues of red, blue, and purple.

The castle you described so intriguingly, Addey, was not open. I caught only a glimpse of it in a heavily wooded area. It did indeed look a "dark and mysterious place." There was no sign of any inhabitant, squinting or otherwise, nor of the dark stairway to which George mysteriously alluded.

That both of us took that same trip gave me a reassuring sense of sharing it with you, Addey. Perhaps we experienced a similar pleasure in returning to picturesque and tranquil Totnes, to which Dartmouth with all its liveliness and seagoing charm could not, at least in my eyes, begin to compare.

7 October 1848

[Addey to George]

At last then you have written. It is time. I began to wonder what could be the reason of your continued silence, and at length, by your letter, I have discovered that it was nothing more than want of time.

So you really did intend to come over on Sunday last, did you? But what a dreadfully thoughtless fellow you are! Dear me! The idea of walking away with Mr. and Mrs. Ladnon, and forgetting that the rest were perhaps impatiently awaiting your return. Incorrigible quite! And then you really did go to Chapel! Astonishing! I declare, but I am very glad of it, nevertheless, and I hope now that you have been once, your attendance will cease to become a wonder.

The weather! (Did I ever write to you without saying something about the weather, I wonder?) Well now, it is wet, miserable, gloomy, dull, sleepy, ill-tempered sort of weather, not shining, not dry, but I daresay you are perfectly aware of the fact already, but I was going to say, that I am very much inclined to be afraid it will be just as bad on Sunday when you have promised to come over, to gladden my heart! And to spend all the day here! Oh – I do hope it will be fine, because I know you hate rain as much as I do.

And you are going to Bristol. I hope you won't be disappointed this time. How long do you intend to stay? A week? I hope you will enjoy yourself, but of course there will be no doubt of your doing that. Oh, how delighted will not your mother be to see you again! And your little sister, Harriet.

I am really afraid now, dear, that I shall not be able to post this today now. Well, you shall have it tomorrow and – we will be reading our letters together – perhaps, for you promised me a good long one on Saturday, you know.

Mother is very well again now and sends her love to you together with Winnie's.

Goodbye – don't disappoint me Sunday morning, there's a love,

Your Little Addey

Addey remarks on his going home to Bristol and says how pleased his mother will be to see him. However, his mother dies on November 8th. Was it sudden or expected? Was he there? There is no mention of this sad event in the surviving letters. There is a long hiatus from October 7 until the letter that follows, but they may well have seen each other during that time, or other letters may have been lost.

22 DECEMBER 1848 HIGHWEEK

Dear Addey,

I daresay you are wondering at my long silence & feeling all sorts of unpleasant things about me, are you not, now? If you could only tell me your mind openly & candidly, would you not say you have seen many things in my conduct lately that displease you, that I am not the same George Virtue of former days. To all of these charges I can only answer by saying my heart is still the same, that has known no change yet, but I have had a great deal to contend with within the last two or three months – events have occurred of which I had never dreamed of. In fact, my whole thoughts & feelings seem changed to what they were when you first knew me. I feel half inclined to be cross with you now & then because you so misconstrue my real sentiments.

There, I'll not dwell on the sentimental any longer. Under present circumstances it would be much better if I were not to indulge in them at all.

Are you going to Bowdon next Sunday?

Pray don't do so unless you wish. I should like to spend my *last* Sunday there though but how shall I know if you will go. I'll venture down to the station Sunday morning & if you are there I can go down with you. If not, I must return again.

You will not *believe*, I suppose, that I have been bothered a great deal since I last saw you at Torquay, nor will you take this as a reason for my not writing. No, I fancy I know exactly how you feel – *you are offended*, is it not so? - - -

Good morning then,
Yours sincerely,
Geo Virtue

SUNDAY EVENING HIGHWEEK

[George to Addey]

What a gloomy day we have had, Addey! I wonder if you expected me at Totnes tonight? I daresay you did. I am in no humour at all for writing & yet I had made up my mind to send you a remarkable long letter & I feel so stupid & dull that I cannot make my old pen cut along at all but I am determined to beat your last. Perhaps I may improve as I go on. You say you are not displeased to hear me talk about myself & I believe you & will take my own feelings in that respect as proof – but I am such a poor miserable unworthy wretch

& you are everything so opposite that the contrast between us is very great. I don't think I ever felt so gloomy & melancholy as I do at present. Shall I open the real state of my mind to you, Addey? I have hardly courage but I feel it is my duty & I will do so.

You have told me on more than one occasion that you truly love me & if you had never said so the many evidences I have seen in your kind conduct towards me would confirm what you have stated. And I love you, too, Addey, dearly, too dearly I fear, for the more I love you, the more I feel my own insignificance.

I almost wish you did not love me. You will ask why? Because Addey, dearest, I am not worthy of your love! I feel I am not! I am sure of it! I often ask myself what it is you can see in me to love but I can come to no conclusion, & when I come to this point I feel there must be a change in your sentiments sometime. If you were more in society where you could see more of mankind, don't you think you would find many men far more suiting to your taste there than me. You may fancy I am mistaken but I think I am correct. If I were wise, or talented, or rich or anything at all to be worthy of your affection, I might think differently but I am not. Then why do you love me?

Addey, do you think you could forget me, if you were to try. Tell me truly if you think you could. I don't mean forget exactly. No – that would be too hard for me to get over but do you think you could get your mind to think of me as an old friend, one whom you knew in your younger days – Try & do this, Addey. I wish (for your sake) you would do so. You ask me why? I will try & explain myself but I scarcely know how to begin. First then, I am growing more & more tired of the Service. I want a change. I feel I shall never be able to support you as I would wish, as long as I stay here. Mr. Carr, our secretary, was once my friend but from a quite trivial circumstance he has taken quite a dislike to me. Mr. Clarke told me this in confidence yesterday, & that he would advise me to try for another course of life for whilst Mr. Carr bore this animosity towards me, I should never do myself any good in the Company's service. Mr. Clarke would not have told me this if he did not mean it. I think he is my friend – but my prospects are blighted now. I thought at one time I should like to live & die in the Service, but I could never do so & know that I was an eyesore to Mr. Carr. When that man once takes an antipathy towards a person, it is deep & inveterate. He never forgets – & damn him, I'll never ask him to.

I have not yet decided what course to take for the future but feel I could do better out of England. Yes, Addey, were not my love for you so strong I would not stay in England a month longer. I feel I can do better abroad – Now, Addey, is it not right & proper that I should wish you would forget me & I think you could do so if you will try! I cannot write longer. My feelings will not allow me & yet I have not said half of what I wish to.

If I go away I *may* return but it is more likely I never shall & therefore I will not harbour the thought. Only tell me you will try & not love me & I shall be *happy* – no, not happy but I shall feel more contented. Oh, how truly forlorn & wretched I feel. God bless you Addey – write me soon.

Geo. Virtue

➢ *A long letter to your beloved Addey at last, George, but what a sad and despairing one it is! Your world has become bleak and uncertain as you struggle to find your place in it.*

On the heels of your mother's death comes disaffection with your job. You do not go into the details, saying only that "a trivial circumstance" has led to your wholesale questioning of your work situation. Convinced your chances for advancement with the railroad are now gone, your anger and pride prevent any thought of resolution.

And because of something you considered relatively minor? I wonder if Mr. Clarke did have your best interests at heart. Did he perhaps take advantage of the grief you were feeling to magnify an incident, perhaps to his own benefit? Or did you misinterpret what he said? You aren't one to anger others, George.

My heart goes out to you as you convey your overwhelming sense of unworthiness to your adored Addey and implore her to stop loving you. You desperately need her solace and affirmation of love. Then you test her further with the possibility of your leaving England as you beg her to forget you.

There is no surviving letter from Addey in response to yours, which, I am sure you would agree, was a lot to respond to. But respond she did in her usual sanguine and stalwart fashion, as indicated by your words below in an undated fragment:

> I have only time to say you are a dear little Addey. I received your letter this morning. I love you very much indeed, and am resuming my old confidence that *you love me.*

PART II

George in London

1849

Such is life – all uncertainty and change

George has left his position at the South Devon Railway Office and has gone to London, where he has found employment with his uncle, who is the head of the family publishing firm, Virtue & Company. Our George is living in Camden Town with his sister, Harriet Lawrence, and her family.

Addey writes the first letter from Torquay. She often visits friends in the nearby seaside resort, staying for weeks at a time. No doubt she enjoys the change of scene and the cultural offerings of what was then called the English Riviera. She recalls it has been a year since they first met.

21 January 1849

Abbey Place
Torquay

Dear George,

Twelve months ago this very night I was first introduced to you dearest. How many happy hours have I spent since then and how few unhappy. Your love has been my endless source of happiness as well as of sweetness. It has beguiled me of many an hour and it has been to me instead of company. But I will make no more confessions, for I think I have said enough about myself, but it was the remembrance of the Ball last year that called it forth. Ah me! I wonder if I shall see you before next year; I will hope so.

Why don't you write to me love? You know I am anxious to hear from you and you know I watch for the postman every day – and you know I am disappointed every day. Don't let it be so any longer. I have had a sort of fancy or presentiment for the last few days that you are ill. Is it so? Write and tell me how you are and what you do and everything about yourself that you can think about, only do write.

How is your sister? And the children? Kiss them for me and I will pay you when I see you and one for the commission.

Last Sunday I intended to go home, and arose early and walked to the station just in time to have the satisfaction of seeing the train by which I meant to go start off at full speed, and left me gazing at it in silent wonderment. However, I tried to make the best of it so I stood still and laughed, and then I turned my back to the station, and indulged myself in a nice long walk alone, the result of which I will favour you with in a separate sheet (if you are good) – so I am going home next Sunday instead of last.

As warm as ever,
Your own Addey

Public and private balls were a way for young people to meet one another. I wish you had said more about the ball: where it was, who introduced you, and whether you caught each other's fancy at first sight. I am left to imagine my own version of what happened. I am thankful it took place at all, or I would not be here to wonder about it.

20 March 1849 — 64 Bartholemew Close, Smithfield

My dearest Addey,

Many thanks for your kind letter yesterday, & the one I received some days before containing the violets. After putting them in water they became quite fresh, & have put me so much in mind of the days gone by.

Oh, didn't I enjoy myself last Sunday. Where did I go, did you say – to Cockfosters? Yes, I started from London in the morning by the Edmonton Omnibus, & arrived just in time for dinner. I had written during the week informing Alicia of my intended visit. Your brother William is a very nice fellow & I like him very much. Mrs. Watson was very kind to me also, but the pleasure was in walking about the garden with Alicia & playing with the young ones.

They are about the same age as *my* two nephews but bigger & stronger. Little Billy & I soon became inseparable friends. He is a dear little fellow. Perhaps it is because he resembles Addey so that I like him, but I certainly think he is my favorite.

Alicia, I am sorry to say, thinks I am thinner & paler then I used to be, but that is natural considering how much I have been confined to the City. My trip on Sunday did me good for I have felt better ever since.

Poor little Jim is on the Isle of France, and of course, he wishes himself home again. He used to work next door to this warehouse. I went there today & the Master shewed me all over the premises, and there was the little stool & apparatus where Jim used to work. The Master gave me a long account of what a nice boy he was when he came there first & and how he got mixed up with bad company & so on. I really did not think I cared so much about him before.

Pardon this digression, dearest, but these thoughts were on my mind & down they are.

I must leave off though I have been longer now than I intended & have not said half enough to be satisfied. I will try to say more next time.

Yours ever,
Geo Virtue

To prevent any mistake, please always call me *Little* Virtue – as I have no wish for the *Publisher* to be reading his *Clerk's* private letters.

George is described as tall but gives himself the middle name Little *to make sure his mail is not confused with that of his uncle. He always makes it a point to use it, and asks Addey to do the same when she addresses letters to him.*

Addey's brother William lives with his wife and children in Cockfosters, a section of north London.

9 April 1849 Camden Town

My dear Addey,

Here I am at last you see, "used up" for a time.

I was taken violently ill at the office on Monday last, & obliged to be taken home in a cab. Doctor says I am in a low fever, & that it will probably be some time before it will leave me.

How very annoying! I am writing this in bed & my old wooden head is in such a dreadful state I cannot move, so I have to guess as to the formation of nearly all my words (& "stunners" they are, no doubt).

I am very sorry Winnie is going away so soon. If I am not well enough to call & see her, will she call upon me, but I know she will.

Oh dear me! I can't write any more, love,

Do write me soon

& believe me
yours ever sincerely,
George Virtue

Addey's sister Winnie is about to sail to India to marry Tom Glanville.

12 April 1849 Bowdon

My dearest Virtue,

Your letter I received on Tuesday, and find that my worst fears are realized in that you are ill. It grieves me much, but I hope you will soon be well again. I wish we had you here. You would soon be able to say, "I am quite well." It would be charming to take you out for a walk on such a delightful morning as this, well wrapt up and leaning on my shoulder for support, and listening to the birds which are at this minute singing beautifully, and anon stopping to admire a flower, which I should instantly gather for you. And then you would thank me with those loving eyes and that sweet smile that I have seen often – but I might run on like this forever, and you would not be a bit nearer. You would still be in London doing all in your power to fancy you were nearly well, but it is pleasant to let our imagination take its will sometimes and ramble where it pleases.

Tomorrow, dearest, is your birthday. Last year I remember you were here and it poured with rain, and now it is fine and will be to-morrow. I like fine weather on a birthday. I think it a good omen. It is telling of brighter days to come: and the weather is now glorious.

I have sent herewith for your acceptance a pair of shoes which I hope will administer to your comfort. They are large I am afraid, but slippers should be loose. Write and tell me how you like them.

Alicia says of course she will call on you if you are still too ill to go to her, but I do hope dearest that such will not be the case.

I wish you were not in London. It does not agree with you, I know it does not, but you are in a nice open part now, I believe? but that horrid old city!

I am quite anxious to know how you are. Write to me as soon as you can, tell me you are better if you can, but don't write too much to fatigue yourself, love.

Mother is quite queasy about you, wondering two or three times a day "how that dear boy is," so just send a line or two. Are you able to leave your bed yet?

Now, my dear, dear George, I must go and pack your shoes or you won't get them tomorrow as I wish. Good bye and God bless you, and may you have many very happy returns of the day and may you see the arrival of each birthday with greater pleasure and more happiness. You will soon be writing to tell me you are all well again, I hope and believe.

Be careful of yourself and be happy.

Yours ever,
Addey

Addey mentions that George's birthday is the next day, on April 13th. He will be twenty-one. She is a few months younger. Her warm birthday wishes for him are sent along with those slippers as she frets about his living in the unhealthy city of London.

Her concern about London was well-founded. It was a notoriously filthy and overcrowded city, plagued by tuberculosis, smallpox, cholera, and typhoid. Dickens' grim descriptions of it were not exaggerated.

George does become ill, though not seriously.

19 April 1849 Bowdon

[Addey to George]

I was very glad, dearest, to receive your note on Tuesday although it was so very short. Remember when you are well again, I shall expect longer letters than you have favoured me with for the last two or three months. And not only longer but oftener. I dare say you will tell me it shall be so but I ask you not to *promise* but *perform,* but *lately,* of course, I know you have been too ill to write much or often. Do you still continue to get better? The typhus fever, was it? Then you have been more seriously ill than I first imagined, but it has had its salutary effects, for we are never ill, *very* ill, without becoming better by it, better in our hearts, for we then have not only the time but inclination to review our past lives and discover the good from the evil and then does this not lead to prayer? And who ever has knelt and offered a fervent prayer to God without rising better and happier for it? Then we are led to form good resolutions for the future which if we seek God's help, we are enabled to keep.

Tell me, love, you are better. Be careful you do not go out too soon or you will risk a relapse which is always worse than the first attack. You cannot be *too* careful. How I should like to see you, but as fate seems to deny that, you must tell me all about yourself.

You will write to me soon, won't you, dearest, and be sure to take care of yourself for my sake. Tell me how you are, *exactly truly,* and let me know soon. Oh, how I wish I were near you.

Good bye darling

Yours
Addey

Empty envelope from George to Addey, postmarked 20 April 1849

MAY
SUNDAY MORNING

My dear George,

I have just been out to look down the road as I used to do sometimes of a Sunday morning, but alas! not with the same hope, for it used to be to see if *you* were coming but such would be a forlorn hope indeed *now.* Ah well, I shall see you coming up the road again yet, shall I not? I don't think this is a wild or unreasonable anticipation to indulge in so I will look forward to the time when it shall be fulfilled; to whatever distance of time through the vista of my imagination I may have to look. Still I can see it, tho' it may be but as a speck each day is bringing it nearer until the speck has increased in size and taken the form of him I love best in all the world. And you are standing before me, really – personally – no phantom produced by fancy, but positively yourself! But I suppose before this picture is realized, we must "wait a little longer." Dear me! haven't I written a great deal of nonsense! Oh my! here they are, home from church already.

Now, my dear George, pardon me that I have not said so before, but I really am delighted that you are so much better. I trust now you will very soon be well. Do, *do* be careful not to get colds, and if it be wet or you are at all fatigued, *don't walk* home for you know you cannot bear *very* much. Thank Heaven I am quite well.

I am sorry dear that I have been bothering you with complaints about the shortness of your letters, but they are much *less frequent,* as well as much shorter. Couldn't you write oftener, dearest? but never write when it is inconvenient or when you are tired. I won't complain again so fear not, and will take what you send with content, nay delight, if – you will only write a little more.

(After dinner) We have just been talking about you. I shall not tell you what tho; don't think it.

Good bye love. Alicia and Winnie are going out, and they are calling me to go with them, and then we are going to church. I hope you are also – are you? So with your permission I will go prepare. I am desired by William through Alicia to say that whenever you feel inclined to go as far as Cockfosters, they will always be very glad to see you, and you are requested to expect no further invitation but to consider this sufficient. Do go down, dear, when time and inclination will permit. By so doing you will oblige

Yours very sincerely,
Addey

MONDAY, 14 MAY 1849 — 64 BARTHOLOMEW CLOSE

[George to Addey]

Well darling! Did you get my *small* story yesterday, as I surmised you would? & where did you go after dinner? I was thinking of you nearly all day, fancying I could see us both strolling leisurely through that most beautiful of all beautiful places, *Bowdon.* This time last year, dearest, I think was about the time I left Totnes for Newton. I little thought then in another twelvemonth how far I should be away from her I loved, but "the time *will* come," as you say, & I hope truly, when we shall meet again, but when? I cannot say. I had made up my mind to come down the fall of this year. I fear though that as I have already had a month's drill I can hardly have the face to ask for leave of absence so soon after my recovery. The change of air *will* do me good, & if I can get away this summer, I most assuredly will, & so dear you may calculate on your "speck" increasing faster than you perhaps first anticipated.

I am much obliged to your brother for his kind invitation.

Write soon dear
& believe me
Yours most sincerely
George Virtue

17 MAY 1849 BOWDON

[Addey to George]

Thank you dearest for your two notes. They made me so happy – they are like yourself, kind and in the old style I love so much, for you used to write to me like it when you were at Newton, when I saw you often. They made me happier after reading them than some of yours lately have done, for I fancied you were growing *cold*. Pardon me, but it is as well to tell you as to think it, perhaps I should not have told you. But dearest I could not help sometimes reading them over and contrasting them with those of former days and surely there is a great difference.

And you really think it probable you may come down this summer. I do hope you may be able – yes, love, the change of air *will* do you great good and I should think your uncle could not object to your leaving, seeing that the month's furlough of which you speak was occasioned by illness, not pleasure. Yes, I have quite made up my mind that you will be down sometime this summer, and I do hope most earnestly that I shall not be disappointed; and so easy is it for us to believe true whatever we wish that I don't think I shall.

So you wish to know what I employed myself about Sunday afternoon – do not let thy vanity listen! I was writing to you. I remembered doing so before breakfast on that same day, before your first note came, and finished it in the afternoon. Where is it? In my pocket and I'm not going to let you see it, so you need not look so cross. I wrote it for my own gratification because it is a pleasure to write to you. There! Smile at that. 'Tis true.

Just as I finished my letter the prettiest of my "pretty cousins" came in with her brother George, a very nice fellow, rather quiet but sensible. After tea we went to Totnes and were caught in the rain. Father came to meet us loaded with umbrellas, as he did once before to meet *us*. Yesterday I went up to get a flower for you. I wish I could do with it as I did with the last bit of heliotrope I gave you – put it in a button hole of your coat.

Twelve months ago this week Tuesday, by the day of the month, you left us for Newton. It has passed quickly. Where will you be twelve months hence, I wonder. I shall be here, I suppose, most likely. Winnie will be in India. Ah well! What changes there are in our destinies in a little year. What great events transpire.

Good bye, dearest. You will write again soon, won't you?

Yours entirely
Addey

As I type your words into my twenty-first-century computer, a device I am unequal to the task of explaining to you – and perhaps to myself as well – I do homage to your writing, which has endured on these pages, tissue-paper thin and fragile. Your words have survived as our all too mortal flesh does not.

Will they last another 170 years, long after I have left this world? And what sort of a place will that be? Something I need not fret about.

May 31 Bowdon

My dearest George,

Well! I declare my hand is shaking with the heat this last day of May. This last month has flown like nothing. I can hardly fancy it was a month ago they said it was "May Day" but I suppose it was – and your arrival is a month nearer! I will own, yes, I *think* I should like to see you. I *really* do, is it not very extraordinary? I think it is, very. Upon my soul, yes, really, you *are* a very nice young man, ain't you?

Poor Jim. I do hope he will come home. It will be so pleasant and perhaps his having been away will do him a great deal of good. If your uncle won't get him home he is very unkind.

Good bye, dearest. Winnie is waiting to take this with her and is getting impatient so I must stop –

so good bye my own love,
Yours ever,
Addey

A fair amount of Addey's news has been left out of this letter as it is about unknown others of her world.

JUNE [UNDATED] BOWDON

[Addey to George]

I am going to write to you, dearest, so long as I can see – which will be but for a short time for it is half past eight.

I always like to tell you all the *news* first but now I have none to tell. In fact we have had excitement enough in our little town for some time to come. It would not do to have many elopements in a year. The good people would soon run mad, or become indifferent, either of which would be a great misfortune.

I do think *generally* pride is stronger than love. What do you think? Winnie does not think so. Tell me your opinion. I think the woman who would sacrifice her pride must be weak and not worthy of the strong love of a man of powerful mind, but if a woman would not give up all, sacrifice everything for the man to whom she has given her heart, and feel her *pride strengthened* by so doing, she would be weaker still.

It is too dark for me to see what I have been writing so good night, dearest, and may happy dreams visit your slumbers and remember your Addey.

Saturday morning. I have just been informed that last night or some part of the day a dreadful accident happened on the line down by Jhira, a man, the stoker, having been killed on the spot by the bursting of the boiler, and another blown high up into a field near by. The deceased has left a wife and six children – dreadful if it be true.

I shall not finish this until tomorrow for you will not get it an hour earlier if I do. Oh, how I should like to see you!

Sunday morning. Well, my own dearest, I must and will finish this now. I am very much inclined to write another and not send this at all, but on second thought, I may as well send the same, that you may see how long I have been writing to you.

Alicia and I went out this morning with the intention of going to Church, but our tiresome old clock happened to be too slow so we were too late and obliged to come home again.

Where are you this morning, I wonder? I wish you were here. You know, dearest, I would rather talk than write to you and rather *listen to you* than do either. I am looking forward to the fall with such pleasure, such hopes and fears, but I think you *will* come. I hope it may be before Winnie leaves us, or there would be a dash of sorrow in the meeting.

George – do you know I think I love you better now than I did when you went away. I am sure I think of you oftener now than then.

The time since I have known you has flown much more swiftly than was its wont. I know of no reason unless it is that I have had a pleasant subject in which to employ my thoughts which I had not before. It seems almost incredible that I have known you for the space of eighteen months! Yet so it is. To you it may not appear so, for you have many other things to share your attention and thoughts, but for me – I have nothing else worth engaging my thoughts, at least for any length of time.

I hope you will be able to go out more. It will be so pleasant, & a change, too, and I know you like variety in all things.

They are calling me to dinner and as I must post this when we go to Church, I shall say good bye at once.

Write to me soon
and accept all the love
of your own Addey

21 June 1849 Bowdon

[Addey to George]

I intended to have treated you with a sheet of larger letter paper this time but I shan't for you don't deserve it for having sent me so short an epistle, but I shall not condescend to grumble about it.

I hope you think I am very good indeed to write to you so soon for I have but just received your note. Shall I tell you then why it is? Because I like to be punctual! Now I am not going to tell you any news whatever simply because I know none to tell, and you may be cross if you like. I don't care a bit what you say or how you look for I shall not see you if you look as black as Erebes.

I am very nearly tired for I have been running about all morning gathering flowers. I am very glad you manage to get some flowers, they must be a source of pleasure to you. Oh dear me I am so lazy.

Yesterday Winnie and myself went in to a public examination of the boys at the grammar school with which we were infinitely amused and gratified.

Now I am going to get the tea. Perhaps I shall not be so cross afterwards.

Well, how are you by this time? I think I am a *little* better.

I suppose you think I am very unreasonable, but you must pardon me, dearest, I know you have not always leisure to write. Even when you write you know I am rather impatient, and I have been expecting to have a letter each day this week, for you have been very regular lately, always writing Mondays. I am not sure that it is a good idea although I like to know when to expect a letter. However, I am very glad I have it at last.

I have just been out to look at the dogs. Vio has seven puppies, such dear little things. It is such fun to see them tumbling one over another and rolling about for they cannot walk yet; they are not strong enough. Shall I get Father to give me one for you? Or can you not so conveniently keep it now as when you were at Newton? Then you said you would like one. There are six *Ladies* out of the seven.

I do *so wish* you were near, love, for it is a delicious evening – so still and so calm – not a leaf astir. Even the birds seem to soften their tunes and sing in subdued voices as if they were afraid of disturbing the general quiet. Oh! It is a lovely evening.

Well, this is much longer than I intended it should be when I began, but I don't how it is when I begin to write to you, I never know when to leave off.

What time, dearest, do you leave your office? And what time do you go in? How far have you to walk to and from home? You have never told me, so please answer all and every one of these questions, and believe me, my dearest George, I am as ever,

Your own Addey

Addey's referring to her visit to the grammar school piques my curiosity as to how she and George were educated.

27 June 1849 London

My dear little Addey,

I am very sorry I have not been able to answer your last before now, but upon my word & honour I have not had time! Monday I was out of town (at Woolwich) all day on business – so I could not do so then, could I? Well then, & yesterday I had to be doubly engaged all day, to make up for the time I had lost the day previous. I hope you will not be angry, dear, will you? There, I can see you are just beginning to smile through your frowns, & feel at rest.

I think you were partly justified in feeling cross at the shortness of my last letter – for I do recollect me well, it was a wondrous short one – but at the time I intended writing again the next day – I did really.

I think I like you to be angry with me sometimes, Addey. Just a *little,* you know, & not for any length of time. That would be awful, indeed. But I don't believe you could remain cross long if you were to try – like April weather, you know.

Yes, I went to Woolrich on Monday, & I feel all the better for my trip. I fancy Uncle will send me out a little more after a bit. I am quite sure it is better for my health than so much sedentary work.

Camden Town is a very healthy spot (for London). It is situated on a slight eminence near the Regent's Park, about two miles & a half from the Close. I am "*on duty*" at 8:15 a.m. & leave about 7:30 p.m. Rather long hours, are they not? But then I have no wish to be "*off duty*" now like I used to, dear, when I would be expecting to see you as soon as I had finished for the day. And all Uncle's people here are very persevering, industrious fellows & I do not feel at all inclined to be number 2 with any of them in close attention to our respective duties. In fact, I give more of my thoughts to business matters now than ever I did in my life. My brothers John, Bill, & Jim, not having been as diligent, as perhaps they should have, act also as an inducement for me to be more active & attentive to make up for their deficiencies in that respect.

Well, darling, old St. Paul's has just informed me that it is 5 o'clock & so that you may get this tomorrow I must now conclude.

Love to all,
Yours ever affectionately,
Geo Virtue

If Governor would keep one of Vio's puppies for me, I should be very thankful for him when I come down in the fall. (I think I should prefer the "son" if no one else has been promised him.)

That's a long day – eleven and a quarter hours with a two and a half mile walk each way.

Eppie, one of the family dog's puppies, makes her first appearance here.

Empty envelope from George to Addey, postmarked 7 July 1849

12 July 1849

Dearest Addey,

I had not time to write to you today in time for the post & for which I am very sorry, as I know you will be expecting a letter from me tomorrow, won't you, dear?

And as you are afraid I am not well, I now with pleasure remove those fears, by assuring you I am quite recovered from my late illness & I think I am much better in health than I have been for a long time. It is true I am not so lively (or thoughtless) now as I used to be. Perhaps I am none the worse for that, as my future course of life & my prospects are materially changed, perhaps I am becoming a wiser (or a more worldly) fellow. At all events I find it absolutely necessary to pay more attention to business if I wish to get on in the world. I feel confident my fate will be much bettered by my removal from the *South Devon Railway Butterflies!!!*

I trust however I shall never become a sordid mercenary wretch similar to many I come in daily contact with – no, Addey, my strong love for you alone will be sufficient to prevent so dire a calamity.

I went with my sister & *dear Alicia* to the Mayflower Theatre on Saturday last & saw a very bad representation of "Dombey & Son" performed, though little Florence puts me in mind of my own little Addey so of course I liked her very much.

Well, it's getting late, darling, & I must away to bed & rise with the lark (perhaps) in the morning & dig away at my garden again soon.

Good night, dear, & God bless you,

Yours ever,
George

Love me *less*, darling, if you wish to see me the most miserable wretch in existence. I know your kind heart too well to be in fear.

➣ *George is adjusting to his new job. He is looking for lodging closer to his office in Bartholomew Close, the address he always uses on his letters. He tries to convince Addey that this is a good move, as she continues to worry about his health in the city of London.*

7 August 1849 64 Bartholomew Close

[George to Addey]

What, are you really coming to London? Oh do tell me when – & how long will you stay? When is Winnie coming to town?

How should you like me to go to New York, Addey, and be away for one or two years – make a fortune, come home – & oh my goodness, what a picture of happiness do I see in the perspective. Yes & then Philip – I don't like to see him there at all – casting quite a cloud over the most brilliant parts of my ideal painting. Oh no, I *ain't* Jealous neither – not a bit of it so don't you be laughing at me, Miss. It's only little bits of unpleasant foreboding coming across my mind sometimes. I love you *too well*, Addey, to know such a feeling as jealousy. You know my mind, dear, almost better than I know it myself – tell me then how I feel.

I remain, dear Addey,
Ever affectionately,
Yours
Geo. Virtue

And suddenly comes a deceptively casual question. You ask Addey how she would feel about your going to New York. Understandably, she is not delighted. She does not subscribe to your notion of its taking a mere year or two to make your fortune and then return to England. You may have wished to convince yourself, as well as her, George. Addey is not as sanguine about such a venture and tells you so.

As for the appearing and disappearing Philip, Addey uses him to tease George, who should know that loving well does not inoculate one from being jealous.

The Compton referred to in the following letter is Spencer Compton, Alicia's fiancé. He is in the East India trade, which takes him away for extended periods. They will marry after an engagement of thirteen years.

AUGUST BOWDON

My dearest George,

I intended to have written this in a very careless sort of manner, but I must ask in the first place, were you *serious* when you asked me what I would say to your going to New York? I hope you were *not!* Have you or are you really thinking about going? As to "making a fortune," I fear it is not so easily accomplished. If you do go, dearest, you will not visit dear old England for *many* years. You say one or two years, but you would not return in so short a time. Compton went out for two or three years and *he* has been away for more than *six* and it is not certain *now* when he will return. Do not go, George – unless you are *sure* it would be better for you.

When is Winnie coming to town? Why, next Monday fortnight, I suppose. Father talks of going also, but I am not sure whether he will or not. I am sure, Love, I don't know when I shall go, not *this* summer I believe, and if you go to America, not next. I shall care very little about it if *you* are not there. No, not even to see Phil, who is there now. He wasn't here more than a week. One may like him and laugh with or even at him, but I should think it would never ripen into love. I should *always* like him, but *never* love him, so you may banish *him* from your pictures of future happiness. And yet sometimes a cloud enhances the beauty of an otherwise too brilliant picture. However, let *him* not be the cloud.

I have just been out looking at the dogs. Eppie is such a dear playful little creature. She doesn't seem like other dogs but bounds along just like a hare. She is so good tempered, but when she is roused she has as much spirit as the others. I think you will like her.

I am half inclined to go to the Torquay Regatta. Shall I? It is on the 26th.

Good bye, dearest, and when you write, answer me all the questions I have asked you. I do assure you I am not at all at ease about you. I have been fretting myself about it ever since I read your note. I know it is very ridiculous of me. And tell me when you are coming down if you know.

Write soon to yours,
Sincerely,
Addey

The Royal Regatta, which is still held every August, began in 1828.

Winnie is finally about to board the ship for India and her marriage to Tom Glanville. George meets Winnie and "the Governor" (as George calls Addey's father) when they arrive at Paddington Station.

4 SEPTEMBER 1849 64 BARTHOLOMEW CLOSE

My dearest Addey,

I suppose you can nearly guess why I did not answer your last letter yesterday – because I went to meet Winnie and the Governor. Yes, dear, that prevented me, altho I might have sent you just a line to say so, but I thought you would not much expect to hear from me before today.

I arrived at Paddington Station just after the train which brought them arrived. Winnie was looking as pretty as ever – only rather tired, of course. The Governor had lost his luggage ticket on the road & was nearly obliged to pay a second time, but after speaking to the Super, he was allowed to pass free of the second charge.

Your brother William was at the station also & we all adjourned to the Inn where William had a conveyance waiting to take them over to Cockfosters. I should have very much liked to have gone with them.

Winnie will come into town again on Thursday, & I anticipate spending a very pleasant evening at Mr. Clampitts. The ship is slated to sail on the 10th but she will probably not do so for some days later. I shall try to get leave for a day in order to shew Winnie about the big city a little. Poor little girl, we cannot shew her too much attention considering how long it will be before we see her again. I am very glad she is able to keep her spirits up so well.

I daresay you will all miss poor Winnie very much, but you must not give way to useless grief & sorrow. After all, seven years is not so very, very long & then at the expiration of that time, fancy her coming home to old England again with five or six little pledges of affection to look after.

I do not like to say I *shall not*, but I am almost inclined to doubt whether I shall be able to come down this fall. Now after saying I would, this is very unkind and provoking, Addey, I know you think so, but I do assure you, the disappointment will be felt quite as keenly (if not more so) by myself. We cannot always do as we wish, darling. However, I can say with certainty that if I don't come down now I shall be able to do so in the early part of next year.

Whoever was it you saw so nearly resembled me? Was he of human mold, think ye, or was it really my wraith? Tell me the day and hour that your eyes deceived you, darling, and I will try and recollect what I was about at that time.

Give my kind love to Mother (Carter & I enjoyed one of her pastries yesterday), Alicia, & my puppy.

Dearest Addey
Ever thine,
Geo Virtue

I can see you all at Paddington Station, which still stands in all its magnificence. After sorting out the upset of the Governor's lost luggage ticket, William takes his father and sister to Cockfoster's in an omnibus.

How sweet to beau Winnie about to see the sights before she is off on the high seas to India. It must have been a merry time and a festive send-off for her.

16 SEPTEMBER 1849 64 BARTHOLOMEW CLOSE

My dear Addey,

We saw Winnie safe on board last night with an understanding that the vessel would sail this morning at 5 a.m.

The Governor & I are going out together tomorrow. I'll write Wednesday.

Yours in an awful hurry,
G. Virtue

As I shall not be here tomorrow I am firing away now to get my work up close.

Love to all

19 SEPTEMBER 1849 BOWDON

My Dearest George,

Just returned from my morning ramble and found your letter waiting for me. Yes, dear, you are right, I would rather wait a day longer and have a nice long one like this. You are a good fellow, George. In fact, *I* don't believe there is anybody like you.

I am very glad Winnie told you about the piano, for if you had not known it, there would have been a "jolly row," but you may set your heart at rest about it, for it cost Father nothing. *I* paid for it. If we had not deceived him we couldn't have had it at all. It emanated from Alicia's very fertile brain and she says if you had confessed the truth, she would never have forgiven you. It is not a *very* nice one, as good as Sarah Taylor's and quite good enough to learn on. I hope to get a better one some day. I commence learning from Sarah next week. I shall have two lessons a week.

What in the name of wonder could you have been talking so *seriously* to Father about! Do tell me. I am dying of curiosity. He has told us you had had a confidential chat but won't tell *me* what about. I think he told Mother, for whenever I ask him she laughs and says, "What do *you* want to know for?" Won't you tell me, love? Ah, if you were here I would be sure to coax it out of you, but you'll tell me, dearest, won't you? You didn't ought to have any secrets, you know!

We had a letter from our dear Winnie yesterday posted in Torquay, the last we shall have from her in England. She is very well and happy, still writes very cheerfully, but sorry am I she has had no letter from us since she went on board. We have both written to her and I sent her the pocket handkerchief intended for her bridal, that cost me so much time and trouble to work, and was obliged to work part of Sunday to finish it, and she has not got it – such a vexing!

I am happy, dearest, that you are well and happy. If my love adds to your happiness, dearest, rest assured it is and ever will be yours. Ah yes, those *were* happy days. Now we must feed upon the past, and not a day passes but I live over in imagination those hours that are gone. Do I love you? You know I did, dearest, and do, but you do not and never can know *how much.*

Satisfy my curiosity about the serious conversation – there's a love – and content thee with the entire love of

Thine own Addey

Addey makes an earnest query about the content of a conversation between George and her father.

That piano you bought, Addey. You had some money of your own? Did you learn to play it as well as your son Herbert did? He played beautifully by ear all kinds of music. I was lucky to have

spent hours listening to him when I was small. He was no older than I am now – myself a grandmother – when I visited him, times I loved then and have treasured since. Long, leisurely breakfasts, walks to the post office along the seawall, watching him perform the morning ritual of lighting his Havana cigar. He had that rare quality of enjoying life and the living of it and gave me a sure sense of being loved and cared for, yet always with a light touch. Somehow this has provided me with emotional ballast, serving me well through some of the turbulent seas of my eighty-plus years.

Diane and her grandfather, Herbert

Torquay

My grandfather Herbert, George and Addey's second son, had made some money during the First World War manufacturing a waterproofing agent for the shoes of those who fought in the trenches. In the summer of 1920, the family went to England with the thought that they might move there. I wonder if their choice of Torquay was influenced by knowing George and Addey had spent time there when they were young and writing the letters.

My grandfather rented a large house on the top of a steeply terraced hill. My mother Isobel was sixteen, and she remembered feeling quite grown-up, as girls of that age often do. One night she attended a ball with a proper and monocled British gentleman. After escorting her home, he made an unintended and precipitous exit, plummeting down the well-manicured turf and leaving great gouges in the lawn. (There was no sign of the monocle, however.)

Knowing that Torquay played its special and often difficult part in the letters, I decided to take a look for myself. I thought it would not be as I had imagined it, but when I arrived and saw the handsome ocean-front setting with its old hotels, its tropical palms and seasonal shops and restaurants, it had a spirit of faded elegance which was much like the picture in my mind's eye.

I stayed in a very English hotel called the Corbyn Head. I tried to find the places Addey had stayed with her friends but was not able to do so. When I asked a guide if Torquay was still popular, he replied wistfully that Spain had become more sought after as a vacation destination because there the sun could be counted upon to shine.

My mother and her family remained for the summer but decided to return to the U.S. She recalled meeting her cousin, Mary Fillingham, who played a critical part in the letters getting to us.

Torquay

I went into the Grand Hotel and had a cup of tea.

24 September 1849

Dear little Addey,

This is only half a sheet but I will endeavour to write close, & after all make it a long letter – condensed.

Let me see now what shall I begin about. Oh, I must tell you how good I was yesterday. I went to a place of worship twice – what I have not done before for a very long time. In the morning I went to Camden Church by myself. In the afternoon I visited a very old servant of Uncle's & after tea went with him to hear the very Reverend Rattenbury, a Wesleyan. Dear me, such an awful row, such groanings & sufferings of the Spirit. I must confess the truth – I felt *very* glad when it was over, or at least when he had finished his sermon, for after that he invited all who had been *moved* by his discourse to remain behind, & he would comfort them in their hour of tribulation. I think the invite was meant more particularly for one or two nice little girls sitting in the Gallery for he looked tarnation hard in that quarter when he spoke. I daresay the poor things did want to be comforted – at all events, *they remained.* Seriously speaking, I think there was far more mockery than true religion in the place – I do not think I shall ever go to a Wesleyan Chapel again.

You will admit you are a *little* curious, will you? You naughty girl, to want to know your father's & my private affairs. Do you very much want to know? Give me a kiss then. If I were near you I would make the price of my secret be at least twenty kisses. Unfortunately, I am too far away at present, bur you will keep them in store for me, won't you? That's a little darling. Oh! I don't think I shall tell you now. Twenty isn't enough, say thirty. Is it a bargain? Yes?

Why, let me see what was it – come a little closer then. I told your father, Addey, how fondly I loved you, that I believed you loved me, & if it met with his approval, would he at some future day consent to our union. I hope, dearest, you will forgive me for having first mentioned this to him without waiting to consult you on the subject. You will forgive me, love, won't you? I told him my future prospects would depend entirely on my own exertions, & that I would never dare to ask for your hand until I felt quite sure of being able to take you to at least as good a home as you would leave.

Your father has consented. It would be useless for me to attempt to tell you what pleasure his sanction has given me. But now I have not asked you, dearest. Will you consent to share your fate with one who so fondly loves you? Be candid, Addey, but be *just*. Weigh the matter well in your mind, consider how many more advantageous offers might be made you. You are yet young & your present love for me might change. What cold wretchedness does that sentence bring to me – but far more wretched should I be if I thought for an instant, I should ever stand in the way of your future happiness.

I will say no more now, write soon, dearest. You may imagine with what anxiety I shall be waiting for your reply.

Ever yours,
Geo Virtue

A more tender proposal I cannot imagine, George. I doubt if you could have phrased it more eloquently had you delivered it in person, and if you had, I would not have had the good fortune to share it. Your words of caution for her to consider your offer carefully, putting her well-being before your own, are just like you, George.

As for your irreverent account of the Reverend Rattenbury's sermon in the Wesleyan service, it reminded me of a remark your son Herbert once made when his wife, Edith, a devout and dutiful churchgoer, asked for some money for the collection. Giving it to her, he remarked, "Fire insurance for another week."

1 October 1849 — 64 Bartholomew Close

My dearest Addey,

What a happy boy your letter of the 25th has made me. Thank you, dear. Thank you. Yes, I did expect a rather favourable answer, but Wednesday & Thursday going by & still no letter – perhaps I did feel a little bit uneasy.

Since Friday I have been forming such lots of new projects, & "building castles in the air" – innumerable. I don't approve of air castle building, though I cannot help doing so. 'Tis so pleasant & you can imagine such pleasing things – nothing like a good foundation & I am *quite determined* now – oh yes – *quite* determined to be such an *awful steady* persevering, economical old pill. You may laugh if you like, Miss Addey. I don't care for your laughing, not a pin. I shall take a couple of nice little rooms near my office & there I'll go home *every* night as soon as I leave work, & read Cobden's *Financial Reform Measures*, & you may quite expect to see GLV looking such a remarkable looking character when he comes down next spring. My coming to Devonshire is a matter of course – it's a great shame I was not able to come down last month as I promised myself, & you, love.

My idea for lodging in the city is that I wish to be near to my business to give it closer attention so that when Uncle George returns from America, he may find his nephew a faithful steward.

And when I am away from Addey, it's by myself entirely I like to be, for then I have her in my thoughts prompting me to do good, & checking me if I think evil, like the dear Guardian Angel she has ever been to me. I often wonder what would have become of me if it had not been for your love, dearest. Really, I don't like to imagine, certainly I should not have remained in London so long *out* of a situation. You told me to *hope on* & I did.

That dreadful old clock! cutting me so short now – just as I was beginning to be so pathetic. Never mind – by the time I write again, I hope to be located in my new establishment. I will give you full particulars then.

Write soon like a dear,
Ever yours,
Geo Virtue

And what a disappointment to miss Addey's letter of acceptance. How fervently I wish it were there. George thanks her for agreeing to be his wife and affirms her continuing good influence on him. Addey is the steadying force in the relationship. Yet George's quick wit and loving nature should not go unnoted. Perhaps most remarkable is his readiness to acknowledge his failings. This is a rare and welcome quality in anyone. I think Addey has chosen well.

I do have difficulty conceiving of George as "an awful, steady persevering economical old pill." That doesn't sound like you, George, even with your newfound dedication to your job.

11 October 1849 Bartholomew Close

My dearest Addey,

I went to Chatham yesterday instead of Friday & that's why you did not get a letter this morning, dear. Of course you expected one. I thought to have had one today also, from you. I suppose I shall hear tomorrow so the pleasure will only be delayed one day.

My trip yesterday did me good, I think. 'Twas a nice clear frosty day & I only wanted little Addey with me to have been quite happy.

About living in the city – your advice & arguments are very good – & kind – as you are always, bless your heart, but there are many reasons for my wishing to live in the city besides those you have mentioned. I sometimes fancy I put them a little *too much* out at Harriet's. Their house is not a large one. When *I know* I am inconveniencing *anyone* it makes me feel quite uncomfortable & wretched. Therefore, until they are settled in a larger abode, I shall move my quarters as soon as I find a decent place. The city, after all, is not such a *very* unhealthy place. See what pains they are always taking to keep it clean, & then you know I frequently take little journeys out of town & that does me good I know & would partly make up for my non-walk morning & evening.

You know, Addey, I wish Uncle to be convinced I am capable of managing this portion of his business myself, singlehandedly. Now if I live near the office I can devote as much time to it as I like & with the shutters closed here & a good fire, I shall be able to find plenty to keep my thoughts employed & when I am tired I can in five minutes toddle home to bed like a good boy & be up in the morning like a lark & at it again. Yes, I have made up my mind to do all this & therefore it's no use your smiling there & shaking your head like that.

Besides there is a little garden here & I can find lots of amusement in it. I shall get you to teach me what flowers to grow & how to plant them. There are several convenient places near here (the Close) but I shall not engage any until I gain *your sanction* so do be merciful. I will promise you this – Should I find my health impaired at all, I will be back to Camden Town or some other salubrious spot. Well, I guess I've nearly worn your patience out about this trifling matter. I ask pardon, dear, & will say no more about it.

Oh don't be getting tired of the piano already after such a fuss to get it. Do go on practicing, there's a dear girl. I'm thinking of learning some instrument this winter. Tell me what you would like me to learn.

Annie desires me to inform you that she thinks Winnie did get the handkerchief as Miss Janett forwarded it to her enclosed in two envelopes, the outer one addressed to Winnie & the inner envelope directed back to Miss Janett in case of Winnie having left. The letter *has not* returned.

Kind love to all
I remain
Dear Addey
Yours ever sincerely
GLV

SATURDAY AFTERNOON BOWDON

[Addey to George]

Well, dearest, you can't get this until Monday. I dare say you are thinking that I might have written yesterday but I couldn't very well.

You will only have to wait a day or two longer, only it will look very like retaliation, but rest assured I did not intend it so.

How much I should have liked to have been with you last Sunday. Allow me to congratulate you on your becoming God Papa. I hope it is a pretty baby for I like pretty children. I should have liked to have seen you.

Oh, I had nearly forgotten – I intend to give you such a scolding so prepare yourself to receive it in all its force. So Sir, you have left your sister's. And you won't tell me where you are, will you? And why, pray? You think I don't know, I dare say, but I *do.* It is because you are gone into the *City.* I know it, I am certain that is the reason, and you can't deny it, and after all your fine speeches about not going there to live if I didn't wish it. Oh George! George – I fear me much there is no more confidence to be placed on what you say than on the promises of the generality of your sex. Tell me if this is not the reason for your refusing to tell me.

George, how pleasant it would be if you were not going to America. I wish you were here. There are so many things I want to tell you about that I cannot write. Well, I must have patience till you come and then perhaps I may say nothing about it. After all, "how little do we know the secret of each other's minds?"

I am to be disappointed again – as I had determined within myself – very foolishly, no doubt – that you could spend Christmas Day at Bowdon, notwithstanding your having told me that you were not coming until after that time.

Write to me soon, dear, and see that you don't forget – either willfully or otherwise – to tell me of your place of residence. If you *do* you must expect no pardon from

Your Addey

6 November 1849 64 Bartholomew Close

My dearest Addey,

I know I am a very bad fellow, for keeping you waiting for this so long. Please forgive me & I will *once* more promise better behavior – Don't look cross, dear, nor pout your lip that way. Now you don't know how many things have arisen to prevent my writing. I was out of town Monday & Tuesday. Uncle George was expected home Monday & I wanted to tell you more about my going away. Getting all our accounts up straight by Uncle's arrival has taken up all my time nearly. I saw Uncle today in his Country House for about a minute, but he was much engaged & I did not broach the subject of my departure to him. Perhaps I shall not go after all, dear, & if I do, you must not grieve, dear, or you will destroy my determination, love, & then I shall be *sure not* to go. Why, 'tisn't far to New York, about 3,000 miles, dear, – only eleven days passage. Fancy now, my going over there, & in five years or so becoming a great man with lots of money saved up & then returning to England to marry my own dear, dear Addey & then – Oh, bother it all, I cannot get further than this. This would be the ultimatum of my happiness. Don't talk about never seeing me again Addey, for shame. The thought of someday making you my wife would be sufficient to keep [*illegible*] in me. I *won't* believe you think anything else would keep me from ever seeing you again.

God bless you dear, darling good girl. How I long to see you.

Yours ever,
Geo Virtue

Write soon, dear, and if Uncle says anything to me tomorrow I will instantly write & tell you.

30 NOVEMBER 1849 BOWDON

[Addey to George]

Tomorrow is the first day of December. Just twelve months ago you went to London. It seems but as last month, and yet what an age since I saw you. Then when next we meet it will be but to say farewell! For how long, must be determined by fate, or chance. It may be for years, and it may be forever! Ah well, such is life – all uncertainty and change – and so it must ever be, I suppose. Only remember you *positively must* spend as much time *as possible* with us before your departure or I'll never – no – never forgive you.

Did Annie Glanville tell you I had been ill? Well, she shouldn't have – only just for about a week and that was nothing, you know. It was quite nonsense telling you who have so much else to think about. However, I am very well now, thank you.

The ship *Dominic* is in and we have had no letter so I suppose now we won't have any until February or March. How I should like to see her.

Now I must get Alicia's breakfast. She is not very well so you will excuse me a few moments, won't you, love? I have only time to just say goodbye. I can't stay one minute longer for it has cleared off and I am going into town.

To my dearest George, write soon to your own

Addey.

Winnie sailed to India on the Dominic.

Empty envelope from Addey to George, postmarked 15 December 1849

1850

We never had such an awful row as this before

January 1850 begins with a flurry of letters, eight of them, a staunch beginning to this third year of the courtship. The greatest number of letters survive from this year. There are nineteen from Addey and twenty-one from George, plus several empty envelopes.

George wrote the first letter on the first day of the first month of the year marking the middle of the century.

1 January 1850 — 64 Bar Close, Smithfield

My dearest Addey,

I have made two ineffectual attempts to write before, but have been prevented each time.

I am not to go to America (at present!!!)

I shall have an increase in salary (which before was scarcely more than a nominal one) & must remain in London with James Virtue, until Uncle has arranged the American business, which will occupy some time. And then I think I shall see my way more clearly to remain in London & not go away at all. Time proves all things.

I hope you have spent a merry Xmas (& if not too late) may you have a happy new year. You little darling of my heart, I am looking forward to spring with much pleasure for then I *shall* see you.

Now Addey dear, you must not complain of the shortness of this letter for I have really more to attend to (just at present) than I can well manage.

We are taking stock & engaging a lot of new men to canvass for the new publications.

James Virtue is a very good fellow and a gentleman!

I spent a pleasant Xmas. I shall not be so busy next week, dear, and then I will write you a "nice long letter." God bless you. Love to all.

Yours ever,
Geo. Virtue

Write soon.
How's Eppie?

January 1850 Bowdon

[Addey to George]

I cannot tell you dearest how happy you have made me by telling me that you are not going abroad. Oh, I am so glad of it! I was beginning to wonder what could be the matter that you had not written and had I not received a letter from you today I should have written to enquire. Are you not glad also dearest that you are not going? Confess now! I know you are.

It is nearly dark so I shall finish this tomorrow, for I am going in to Totnes this evening to take Miss Bennett a boquet [*sic*] for she is going to a ball tonight. I shall stay and help to dress her perhaps as I did for a like occasion two years ago this month. Do you remember it, love? Ours was a singular meeting, I think, all things considered. Ah well! I wonder if it would never have been as it is if we had not gone to that ball! Ah those were pleasant days. I should like to live over a few of them, I think, and the walk in the snow in the morning. The ground is white now as it then was. I don't mean to include that walk in one of the days tho: although your arm would be some use to me this evening in walk for 'tis very slippery. However, I have learnt to do without it and so I must tonight. Goodbye dearest for the present.

Well I have been to Miss Bennett's and she is very much disappointed that I was not to be of the party but I was not.

I am very sorry darling that I cannot write a very long letter now but I hope I will next time, and you will too for you said you would.

Goodbye, my own George. Pardon the brevity of this letter. Oh, I am so happy!

And you are looking forward with pleasure to the spring and am not I! Ah well, I must go. Let me go! as you used to say. Be assured of the constant love of

Your own Addey

➢ *You must have taken an immediate fancy to one another to have taken a walk in the snow the next morning. How I wish Addey had elaborated on their "singular meeting."*

7 January 1850 — 64 Bartholomew Close, Smithfield

My dearest Addey,

I promised you a long letter this time I know, but I do fear me I shall not be able to fulfil my promise, however I'll not leave off 'till I'm obliged to.

So you really are glad I am not going to America are you? (bother! here's my tea now). Well, I thought *you* would not be very sorry, perhaps I am rather pleased also, but yet I felt it as a sort of disappointment too. You know, my dear, I had made up my mind on the matter as to how I should act & had drawn out my future plans in such a pleasing sort of perspective (I need scarcely say what a very conspicuous form you had in the whole) that altogether I was put a little out of the way when I found how truly I had been "building castles in the air." 'Tis all gone away now tho, & my mind is once more made up to remain in Old England as long as I can. With all my fine plans & prospects about going away, I must admit I had sundry doubts & misgivings of by no means a pleasing or satisfactory nature.

I am going to be very economical & saving this year, of course I *am already steady.*

Yes, my own darling Addey, & I shall always thank you for my being so. Dear me, I often wonder what would have become of me by this time if I had never known you. God bless you. You are & always will be my guardian angel.

Now I'm very cross. I must either disappoint you again & finish this tomorrow or leave off at once. I very much wanted to have a long chat with you today. Never mind, dear, you will pardon me, won't you, like a little darling as you are.

In haste,
Yours ever sincerely,
Geo Virtue

Write soon
Love to All
How's Eppie (No. 2)

[The word "mystery" is written on the inside flap of the envelope.]

10 January 1850 Bowdon

[Addey to George]

Did you expect a letter from me today, dearest? I intended that you should have had one but was prevented from writing to you yesterday.

On Tuesday we were surprised by Mrs. Piper and Bess. And a great wonder that I am not at present writing from Torquay, for the aforesaid ladies came over with the full and entire conviction of being able to prevail on us to return with them. In fact, they came to fetch us, but Alicia could not go, for she is suffering from a severe cold. I could have gone and was excited by a desire to go, but unfortunately and greatly to my mortification Mother could not be prevailed on to consider the proposition with anything approaching its favour. So I was compelled rather reluctantly I confess to refuse the invitation but not before we had obtained a promise from Mother that I shall go very soon.

What a pity it is dear that airy castles should generally end in airy nothing. I am not sorry your American castles are, tho, I too had built my castles, which were all blown away when you spoke of going away. Now I shall begin to build them again with renewed hope and pleasure. I am half inclined to tell you why I am so very glad that you are not going. On second thoughts I don't think I shall. I shall only say that the "course" of our love is more likely to run smooth at home. I should not have said this much if you still expected to go. Now I suppose you are beginning to fancy that there is some mystery in all this but it is not so. We should have loved each other as much in America as in England, but it is much better for *my* happiness as it is, I know. And I think I may venture to say for *yours* also.

How do you like your lodgings dear? You have not told me. If you are not comfortable don't stay, there's a love. You said you would be more comfortable with your Uncle James. Are you going there?

When do you expect your brother James home? When did you hear from brother Bill, and how is he? Give my love to him. I should so like to see him again. He is such a favorite of mine. I very often smile at the remembrance of the evening he was here and his "sing Winnie dear!" to Winnie up by the old gate, where she sang Gestal and Larry Drew saying he would like Winnie to sing to him when he was on his death bed. Odd fancy, eh? Oh, talking of him puts me in mind of a bit of news I heard the other day. It is that "Mr. Guihard Drew's two sisters are coming to Totnes to open a school." I can't answer for the truth of the report, and I hope it is not true for I don't think another school will succeed for there are quite enough already for the town.

Have you seen Annie lately? Poor girl. From what I can glean from Father and her own letters I think it must be a horribly gloomy place where she is living, is it not? And Jem is not of a temperament by any means likely to enliven its gloom or to render her (or anybody else himself included) happy. It must be such a change indeed for her from what she has always been accustomed to. For hers was such a cheerful home at Stoke when her father lived. Poor girl, it is a great pity for her.

How is Eppie? Oh, she is very well and so lively! But I am vexed with her for I can't get her to eat anything. She is so dreadfully thin, that I don't know what to do with her. Alicia says it's the exercise she takes that keeps her so but she eats so very little. Isn't this a long letter?

I hope you are pleased you shall have it tomorrow.

Now goodbye dearest,
write soon to your own Addey

17 January 1850 — Bowdon

[Addey to George]

I have a great mind to give you a good blowing up, nearly as long as I used to write, indeed. I am sure it was *quite* as long, if not longer, and now sir may I ask if your letters now are *ever* so long as they "used" to be when I used to have *two* during the week instead of *one*? No indeed they are not, 'tis very true. You manage to get to the end of the sheet by dint of stretching out the letters of the words as well as the words themselves. No, no, sir, none of your insinuations until you improve yourself. *Then*, if mine are unusually short you may have some right to complain. You'll plead want of time, I know, but 'tis all nonsense. If you felt *inclined* to send me a long letter you would soon make *time*. There I mean it, remember.

I have just written to Winnie. I was interrupted yesterday when I had arrived this far by a gentleman who came to see Father, but as his request could not be granted without my consent, he had the grace to inform me of his mission and I (rather reluctantly) refused. He is such a nice fellow that if I had not thought I knew "a nicerer" I should not have been able to refuse his request. Now I shall not tell you what he wanted so you needn't ask! Neither am I going to explain what I meant in my last letter either. Perhaps I *may* tell you *some* day but I shan't now. Oh, yes, you may call me cross if you like. I don't care for that but I was told the other day that is was a "thing impossible" to make me cross. You know better than that, eh? I was yesterday a little as the commencement of this very loving epistle will show. Oh, wouldn't I torment you if you were here. I feel just in the humour, but if I felt so ever so much and you here to practise on, I could never hope to equal you in the art of teazing. So you may comfort yourself with that.

I heard a bit of news the other day that did make me laugh so. I have a half a mind not to tell you. However, I think I will. Do you know the Misses Elliott of Little Hempston? Well, the sixth daughter (there are 8) has been engaged to a gentleman living at ___ for a long time. This Christmas he has been on a visit to them. While he was there he quarreled with his lady love. The seventh sister was asking him about it and he said he did not care, in fact he was rather glad of it for Caroline was a very bad temper, and he would as soon marry her as Carry, to which the young lady answered that he was quite right. Caroline was a very bad temper and she was tired of her too and tired of staying home and concluded by saying "if you would as soon marry me as Caroline, I would rather!" So it was settled between them that the marriage was to take place last Sunday and kept secret from the family. So she came in to Totnes and invited Lizzie Taylor to be her bridesmaid and she would send a fly for her. But unfortunately for them, Mr. Elliott by some means heard of their intentions and went to the minister and forbad him to marry them, which they did not discover until they were at the church. And while they were expostulating with the clergyman, the lady's brother and another sister's lover came to stop the proceedings, when there was a desperate fight in the church, in which the bride elect joined with hearty good will (they are all famous for their pugilistic qualifications) and with her lover gained the victory (with no more serious loss than her bonnet). And springing into the gig that brought her brother, followed by this lover, drove at full speed to the station where they took a train and went off to where I believe they concluded the ceremony! She still wore on her head the wreath of orange blossoms (that she had on under her bonnet) which was surmounted by her lord's traveling cap, which had superseded the bridal bonnet. The young lady afforded the gentleman at the station a fund of amusement by her incongruous dress, for besides the cap and flowers she wore a thin white dress and blue satin jacket. Oh, how terribly cold she must have been. I think she needed his great coat as much as his cap.

The poor disappointed bridesmaid was obliged to return as she went, alone in the fly. What do you think of the affair? She fought for him, however, and won him too. Would you like your bride to fight for you?

How I should have liked to have seen you on Sunday skating on the Serpentine! Dreadful! It must have been much colder in London than here for we have had no such frost as that. What will you say to me dear if I knit you a pair or two of mittens to keep your hands warm while writing. Spencer used to wear them when he was in England and found them very comfortable things. Will you wear them if I knit them?

I like your cousin, Bessie. Who is it says you may know a person's character or disposition by a letter. Now I think I know her better by her letter than by anything you could have said. And I like her but is she not rather – rather ceremonious? You know, isn't she?

We yesterday received a circular for a ball. But I suppose I shall not go. I should rather like to but if I were to go I am afraid I should be thinking of a certain gentleman who shall be nameless all the time and wishing him there and so not enjoy myself very much.

Somehow I don't like parties so well as I used to. They are tiresome to me now. Oh, dear me and they used to be my greatest delight. I shall not say what is *now*.

I wonder if you will spend your birthday at Bowdon? Do you think it likely?

Well I think surely this is as long as they used to be, is it not. Now sir I do hope *you* will write longer letters than you have favoured me with lately. Will you love, and then I will try to please you in everything, and I don't think that you are very difficult to please, are you? . . .

What is the name of the people with whom you lodge and how many and what sort are the family composed of? I am glad you are getting more reconciled to them . . .

Give my love to Annie when you see her and tell her she owes me a letter.

Now I won't write anymore.

Only Eppie is better. I don't think she will be ill, she is so lively. Poor little thing. 'Twill be dreadful to [*illegible*] her life in a city.

Goodbye dearest,
Yours ever,
Addey

Write soon darling.

Addey's rendition of the exploits of the Elliott sisters is a lively bit of Victorian hilarity.

THURSDAY MORNING BOWDON

[Addey to George]

Now then dearest, before I do anything more I'll write to you for I do assure you I am very busy indeed and this is the day for visiting my music mistress. I take two lessons every week.

Did your father arrive and how is he? Does he look better than when you last saw him? Then I remember you said he looked very ill, and was much altered.

I cannot but feel very much flattered dear by the desire you evince to gratify my wishes, even when relating to yourself, and I heartily thank you, and since the decision is left to me, I certainly would rather you would *not* live in the city for I feel quite sure that a constant residence in the city would have very ill effects on your health generally, even if it did not make you very ill. So I would say live as *far away* as possible from it and now I am on the subject I will lay strict injunctions on you to take *very great care of yourself* and be sure you don't get *wet*, or at any rate don't keep your wet clothes on you longer than you can possibly help. Now I dare say you are laughing at me for all this, but I don't care, what I say is *quite right*. Do you keep a dry pair of shoes at the office? Because if you don't, *you must*. Now I *order* this and beg you attend to it. And *always change* when your feet are the *least damp*. Now won't you say I am a little fidget but I think I am quite a sensible young woman!!

You are such a darling and I can't afford to lose you and if you are ill I should not be near to nurse you, you know.

I cannot tell what to say about Eppie. She is terribly rude and unmanageable but so very lively. She has lost her brother, poor dear. Father sold him yesterday for a sovereign. She is fretting. She has a very poor appetite. She eats scarcely anything. You have no idea what a favorite she is with Mother. I do believe it is only because she is *yours*. She is very well and a nice little thing, but I am compelled to say she is not *very* pretty. There I'm sure that's a lot about Eppie. She is very fond of me.

Am I not good to write to you so soon, but I dare say you expect it, and I must own you deserve it and all my love besides, which I am half afraid you have already.

However, I can't help it, and as far as that goes, I wouldn't if I could.

Goodbye my own dearest.

Yours ever,
Addey

Everybody's love

I have just received a letter from Annie and she says – but I shan't tell you what she says about *you*. She says you play the flute very nicely. Why didn't you tell me so? I thought you had given up practicing on it. If it doesn't hurt you, dearest, continue it for I like the flute so very much. It is almost the most beautiful of any I think, and then we shall be able to play together, eh? It will be really delightful. Oh, yes play the flute if *it does you no harm*. Now love I must write to Winnie for it must be posted today. I shall write to Annie again soon for I like her letters very much.

Goodbye love,
Your own,
Addey

write soon

29 January 1850

64 Bartholomew Close
Smithfield

My dearest Addey,

Remember me to all your cousins and tell Master Richard I shall feel much pleasure in making his acquaintance next spring when I come down. But I say Addey you mustn't be too fond of Dick. Yes you may then for 'tis a cousin's privilege as you say, & in my opinion a perfectly natural one. I say, do you think I am a jealous fellow? I don't know if I am or not, in fact I feel proud to think you have never yet given me cause to feel the goadings of the green-eyed monster.

Well now you are a kind dear little soul to so easily concede to my wishes, & to convince you of my gratitude I am already in treaty with an old lady close by here for a parlour & bedroom. I shall be able to pay more attention to my business & am quite sure 'twill be infinitely better in every respect. I had half engaged to live at Pimlico prior to this, but on second thoughts I fear I should find it too great a distance. However, in the summer I may yet reside there. The walk thro the park every morning will do me good no doubt.

I am looking forward to the spring with much pleasure. Oh by the bye you asked some time ago if I should spend my next birthday at Bowdon.

I could do so I think, but is not May a better month to come down? My last birthday wasn't a very merry one, & yet I remember I did not feel particularly unhappy. Your kind consoling letter, all thoughts on the fever & everything else of an unpleasing nature, upon my word, I do most verily believe there was as much credit due to you for my cure as for the doctor. Knowing dear little Addey to be feeling for me & wishing me well, who could remain ill I wonder.

I am glad you thought my last an improvement; 'tis encouraging. Wait till I get to my new residence & then won't I try your patience.

Well goodbye love. Write soon and believe me dearest Addey,

Ever thine,
George

Love to all. Is Eppie better? I was dreaming about you and her and Bowdon all Sunday night.

1 February 1850 Bowdon

Dear George,

You will be very glad, dearest, to learn that we have heard from Winnie, not from India, but from the Cape, where they expected to stay two days. I wonder if she saw your brother. Do you think it likely? It was such pleasant news. She was enjoying herself so very much. Agreeable company was aboard and beautiful weather though it was very rough in the Bay of Biscay where they were four days. Many of the gentlemen were Irish and a constant source of amusement, the greater part military men and those who are married had their wives with them. They spent their evenings when fine on deck dancing, singing, chatting, laughing etc. She said she would be rather sorry than otherwise when they would arrive at Madras. She seemed to be in excellent spirits and delighted with the voyage.

She had formed an intimacy with a Miss McLeach who would be a near neighbor of hers.

That is very pleasant, is it not? She sends her love to you. The week previous to the arrival of her letter I received one from Tom. He was about to start for Madras to meet her, and was very happy in the anticipation of meeting his wife. We were so glad to get her letter and if the Fates be propitious to receive a full account of her arrival and marriage at the end of this month, or if not, next. I expect she has been Mrs. Glanville some five or six weeks.

I am very glad indeed that you think you will be much more comfortable with your old lady hostess. I am anxiously waiting to have my patience tried. I have a goodly stock, and I don't think it likely your letters will ever be too *long*.

Yes, dearest, I do think May is the best month decidedly for visiting, however much I may wish to see you before. I am glad you have mentioned a definite period for your visit for I like to have something to look forward to. Looking forward to the spring is not so pleasant as looking forward to May.

My dear George, you must not expect your mittens yet, for it has made me very cross to think I could not get any wool for them in the town, but Alicia is going to Torquay on Monday, when she will get some. I think the cold weather is nearly all gone but then they will be useful next winter, won't they? And it strikes me that once you have tested their comfort, you will make me knit you some every winter, and won't I do it with pleasure.

Now my own dearest, I will say to you goodbye,

Write soon to your own
Addey

Valentine's Day Bowdon

[Addey to George]

I did not get your letter till today, dearest, so it served for a Valentine, and I could not have one to please me better, for it came from *you*. However, I consider that I owe you an apology although you don't know it for I was scolding you in my mind all day yesterday for not having written.

Mother was taken very ill yesterday morning and still continues so. It is dreadful, love, to be stalking about the house in such sad silence and nobody to speak to for Alicia is not yet returned. It makes me quite melancholy, and that is not very usual for me to be. However, I trust Mother will soon be better again. It is so unusual to have sickness in the house.

I was dreaming of Brothers Bill and Jim last night and I thought that Bill said you were "terribly sulky" and the least thing made you angry! Dreams always go by contraries, my dear, and I know very well that there is nobody in all the world half as good as my own dear, dear George. I fancy I can see Brother Bill's quiet smile and wicked twinkle in his eye.

Spring is coming dearest (and so is May) for I gathered three primroses today. What a beautiful season is spring, the happiest in all the year. It is the season of *hope.* I am not going to moralize here, but will keep all that for some future time – which will please you, I know.

Do all or any of Jem's friends have beards like himself? If so, I shall never like any of them. I hate *beards!*

Alicia has just requested me to send her love to Mr. Virtue, so she guesses to whom I am writing for I haven't told her.

Now my dearest George, I must go up with Mother's supper so I will only stay to reassure you of the unalterable love of

Your little Addey

Write soon

I share Addey's distaste for beards. What would she think of today's ubiquitous stubble?

26 FEBRUARY 1850 64 BARTHOLOMEW CLOSE

Dear Addey,

Just 5 minutes to post time.

I've been to Guildford & only now returned. I should like to tell you how I liked my journey & what a nice old fashioned place, something like Totnes but not so large.

Thank you for the violets & your good long letter. I didn't receive it till Monday morning, though I felt sure you had written. Bless your heart, the 95 days are slipping round, Addey.

I can't stop another minute. Pardon this, Addey, upon my word, 'tisn't my fault.

Ever yours,
Sulky

Love to all
Next shall be longer

4 ABBEY PLACE
TORQUAY

My dearest George,

I suppose you are surprised to see that I am once more at Torquay but I am nevertheless on a visit at present to the Misses Crockwell. I wish you were here. It is such glorious weather and the place is very gay.

Do you know that we have heard of Winnie's safe arrival at Madras. When she wrote she was to be married on the following Wednesday, the sixteenth of January, so I suppose we may safely call her Mrs. Glanville. One of the young ladies who went out at the same time received a letter to inform her of the death of her lover. Poor girl, that must have been dreadful indeed and she had gone so far. It was worse if possible than if she had been in England. How very bitter it must be to mourn the death of those we love, perhaps worship. I cannot bear to think of it, George. What could I do if *you* were to die? Die too, I think.

Sara sends her "best love" to you. I said I would give it to you since she wished it, but I told her that I didn't know what business she had to send it, do you? She is gone to attend to her pupils.

Carter's mother has his portrait. It is so exactly like him. There is much pleasure I think in looking at portraits of our friends. I like them, don't you? One can almost fancy it is the one beloved instead of only a senseless painting. Besides it is delightful to recall the look of some particular time, the expression of some treasured moment. It is such a delightful aid to memory. I often wish I had yours, love, not that I ever forget you, you know.

Well, darling, I can't write any more now for I am tired. I staid up late last night and I am not used to late hours. I am not very well and moreover, Margaret is practicing and it distracts my attention. So my own, you will excuse me, won't you?

Write soon and direct for me to 4 Abbey Place.

Ever as ever your own,
Addey

Winnie's safe arrival in India was an auspicious beginning to a happy marriage – which must have been encouraging to Addey.

Empty envelope from George to Addey, postmarked 13 March 1850

15 MARCH 1850 16 VICTORIA PARADE

[Addey to George]

Thank you dearest for the expressions of confidence in your last letter. I knew you would not be angry with me for I knew I was not wrong.

I did *not* go to the concert on Monday night last, not because I thought it wrong but because I was deluded by false hopes, for the girls said they were going so of course I intended going with them until it was quite time to go when I found out they had changed their intention and consequently I was disappointed and wasn't I vexed! Never mind. I shall hear them in London some time, I dare say.

You did not tell me, love, what the amateur performance was to be in which your cousin took such a prominent part. Were you pleased? We often go to the theatre. The performers are not first rate but very good for the country. We are going tomorrow night when it will be patronized by the Duchess of Bedford.

You see, dearest, from the date of this letter that I am at present staying with Bess who sends her love to you. Please direct your next letter here. I think I shall go home next week.

Bess is waiting for me to go out with her, so my own love, I am compelled to say to you goodbye, much against my inclinations, but if this is not posted now you won't get it till Monday.

Be assured, my own beloved George, you are constantly in the thoughts of your little Addey, however I may *flirt*.

Goodbye, dearest. Write soon.

9 April 1850 Castle Inn

My dear George,

Have you been expecting to hear from me before? The fact is I have not been in a humour for writing to anybody, not even to you and I am not quite now. Do you wonder why? I have had a desperate quarrel with Bess and when one falls out with one's friend (or *supposed* friend) one cannot easily get quiet enough to write. I'll tell you when I see you, if you are at all curious. Suffice it to say, she has insulted me beyond endurance and has striven to "rob me of my name." And in fact has said things without the slightest foundation that cannot possibly be forgiven and I will *never* speak to her again.

I have made a fresh acquaintance in a Miss Spark, a sister of Mr. Spark, a friend of mine. Yes, you would like her. She is a merry, lighthearted, good-tempered, cordial *English* girl. As for her brother I shall not attempt a description of *him*. At present he is stage-struck.

I think, dear, you had better direct my next letter to Bowdon for I *think* I shall go home this week.

I cannot write what with the bad pens and altogether you must not be angry because you have no need, but write again soon, and believe me,

Your Addey

The usually imperturbable Addey has a grievance with one of the Torquay girls she visits, Bess. She does not elaborate; however, she is writing from an inn, which suggests a change in her lodgings.

12 April 1850 — 64 Bartholomew Close

My dear Addey,

What have you & Miss Bess been kicking up a row about, I wonder? If *you* can spare time you cannot give *me too* detailed an account of the whole proceeding, but I hope it is not really of so serious a character as you have been persuaded to believe in the first instance.

I hope this letter will find you safely returned to dear old Bowdon. I like writing to you there much better than at Torquay, although I must say but little this time for it wants but a few minutes to post time.

We had a severe thunderstorm here this morning, the rain descending most copiously, placing my small garden, flowers & all, in much jeopardy of being washed entirely away. However it is cleared away fine now and I daresay we shall have some sunny weather.

Well, Addey, let me go. You shall have a much longer letter next week & I do trust I may look forward to more lengthy ones from little Addey.

God bless you my dear Addey.

Ever yours,
Geo. Virtue

Will you write soon?
Kind love to all
Is Eppie quite well?

Empty envelope from George to Addey, postmarked 22 April 1850

30 April 1850 Bowdon – in bed

[Addey to George]

Why do I not write? I daresay you are in a state of wonderment. Well, have patience and I will endeavor to explain. You must know in the first place that your letters did not reach me until last Thursday from the fact of my not arriving home as soon as I was expected, and Alicia instead of forwarding them to Torquay, kept them in daily expectation of my arrival until the very day I came home when I learned she had that morning sent on *two* letters from George.

Now you see I am writing this in bed which I have not been able to leave today, but thank you, I am better than I was.

Are you curious to know what Miss Godfrey and I have fallen out about? Well, it is a long story, in fact too long to write a full account of. I was thinking you might have heard of it from Annie. It is altogether a very unpleasant affair, dear, yet it is good for one to find out one's real friends from those who only pretend to be. I will never speak to her again, if I can by any possibility avoid it. The quarrel is not only with her, but with *all* the girls. When you come down, George, I will tell you all about it.

I made a long visit at Torquay, didn't I, and enjoyed myself very much, I assure you. I have promised to go again when you come, dearest. I said I should go there to meet you but I don't think I shall. Alicia says she would not if she were me, so I suppose it would not be right.

It's getting dark. I can't see any longer so I must put this away now.

Tuesday morning:

Still in bed but I do hope I shall be allowed to get up today. I am tired of staying here.

We had another letter from Winnie on Tuesday; she is so happy and well and likes the place very much. In fact she is quite delighted with Tom and with everything.

Only one month more, dearest, before we shall meet after an absence of nearly a year and a half. What a long, long time it has been! I won't allow you to stay away from me so long again. 'Tis dreadful! I have such hundreds of things to tell you. I dare say I shall forget a half of them. Oh, but I forgot. You are angry, are you? I should like to look at you just now that I may see how you look when you are not pleased. Let me see, did I ever see you angry? Yes, I think I had that pleasure once in the garden. Do you remember?

Will you write soon to Addey?

9 May 1850 — 64 Bartholomew Close, Smithfield

My dear, dear Addey,

How can I begin to write after behaving so badly as I have. I really don't know what to say. Perhaps I thought you would write again as our last letters crossed each other & you tell me to speak truly, I positively began to think *myself* the ill-used individual & you were the aggressor for keeping me so long in suspense. These were all extremely shortsighted & selfish ideas I now frankly admit, but nevertheless, such motives as these were in truth the cause of my silence. In fact, this afternoon I had purposed writing you a very long, sober, serious kind of letter accusing you of trifling with my feelings & all that sort of thing, when lo, this morning I received this kind letter from you wherein you perfectly justify yourself & I the self-imagined martyr, find myself having acted as you most truly observe, a very unkind & selfish part. Indeed I hardly know how I can put matters right now. I'm sure, dear me, I ought to be very serious now, Addey dear, yes I'm aware of that, love, 'tis no joking matter, but don't look cross, Addey. Smile now like you used to & say you forgive me. We never had such an awful row as this before, did we! 'Twas all my fault, Addey. I'm a pretty good sort of fellow in some things but I was in a bad disposition & I entertained all at once a most morbid idea, all that you loved someone at Torquay better than me and that was why you didn't write and so it came on darker and darker till I worked myself into a remarkable live specimen of the "Green Dragon" and a man can't be responsible for what he does or does *not* do, but then you will forgive me, love, won't you? No, very well blow me up then, every letter till I come down, as much as you like, darling, quite hot & strong, you know, & when I come down why I'll kiss you all the more for it.

I have no reason to doubt I shall come down when I promised & will go to Southampton first & will then take the rest of my journey by sea or land as I find best.

I shall leave London early in the morning of the 25th & calculate being at Bowdon sometime on the Sunday following.

Goodbye my own dear Addey. The idea of losing you and loving someone better is so preposterous I cannot possibly conceive it.

Write soon, Addey, won't you?!! and believe me ever,

Yours most affectionately,
Geo. Virtue

The person who told you I loved another ceased to be a friend in telling you, even were it true, but as it is an unfounded & *damned* lie, the party, whoever they were, is an enemy & a knave.
How is Eppie?

> *Not hearing from Addey ignites George's dark imaginings, and he believes she has forsaken him for another. What can only be described as a fit of jealousy turns him into a self-admitted "remarkable live speciment of the 'Green Dragon.'" However, in his usual way he makes no excuses and acknowledges his bad behavior as entirely his fault. George is particularly susceptible to such downswings when he doesn't hear from his beloved when expected, but a calm word from Addey puts him back on track.*

18 May 1850 Bowdon

[Addey to George]

Well, love, I think we are at cross purposes, don't you, for our letters are constantly crossing each other on the road. I am very nearly tired of writing for I have written a long letter to Winnie and have sent your love to her. If you had been here you should have written to her. Only one week more and you will be here. I wonder very often if you are at all altered in any way. I *fancy* you are, are you? I am very much. You won't know me, and you can't tell how cross I am become. I don't care for anything or I think anybody, oh now you needn't flatter yourself. You are not an exception so you need not think it. And so you will see when you once more put foot on Bowdon. Oh dear me, won't I serve you out, I'll teaze you as much as ever I can. And you will leave me quite astonished at my ill temper, for I don't think you think me as bad as I am. I wish you were here that I might begin at once, for I am as cross as I can well be now.

Have you decided yet on the manner of your coming, or must you go to Southampton?

Mother has just desired me to request you to get for her and bring with you a bottle of liquid glue for we can't get it here. Don't forget now.

Oh, I must tell you a bit of news. You remember Mr. Elliott at the Newton Station? Well, he has married an heiress with a fortune of £300,000! Isn't he a lucky fellow? Don't you envy him? They are gone to New York. A most romantic affair altogether.

Well, it is useless to try for I *can't* write and I *won't* write now! You may frown and look as angry as you please. I'll *talk* to you as much as ever you like next week, only next week, I can hardly realize it and you have been away for a year and a half nearly. I hope it will be fine weather while you are here. I think it will.

Write, there's a love. I shall have *two* letters from you next week, one to say when and by what train you are coming. If you do disappoint me, woe be unto you!

I press my lips to your forehead and say adieu (*fancy* it you know and it is done).

Your own always.
Addey

Addey's request that George bring a bottle of liquid glue for her mother is an appealingly concrete detail. Our lives are often punctuated by bottles of glue.

George visits Addey in Devon May 25th through June 5th. Their later letters give no hint of what they did that week.

7 June 1850 64 Bartholomew Close

My dearest Addey,

Here I am you see, home safe & sound & with plenty of back work before me to get up as you may suppose.

You would like to know my career after I left you Tuesday afternoon, wouldn't you, love? Well then, I'll try to remember all the places I went to & the people I saw worth remembering.

Eppie had a strong inclination to return with you to Bowdon & I being quite of an opposite turn of mind, of course, had some difficulty to get her ladyship to the station, where I arrived just in time to save the train.

I spent a few hours *rather* pleasantly with Morgan. I say rather for I could not help thinking, dear, how far happier I should be with my dear little kind & affectionate Addey. I am an obstinate, selfish, stupid sort of fellow, Addey. I used to think so, but now I am sure of it, love, & you think so, too, don't you? God bless you, my dear girl. I have thought many times since I left you, that you more than once seemed almost to doubt if I really loved you. Tell me if you did not? But I shall not finish my story tonight unless I look sharp.

From Dawlish to St. Thomas where Eppie & I were welcomely received by Mr. & Mrs. Batt. At Exeter we slept till 5 next morning & then off by first train for Bristol. Father & Tom were home. Ted was at his business & Bill out of town (nor did I see that worthy individual at all though he knew by my letter that I would be in Bristol at the time specified in my note to him).

And now I must tell you a story the fact of which has caused me much trouble & anxiety. Miss Eppie gave me the slip just as we got to Tom's house & made off with all speed to Caversham Park. After a useless chase of three hours, I was compelled by darkness to give up. I slept at Reading last night in the hopes of finding her & I was partly successful – for I saw her coming down the road towards Mullen's (Tom's) house accompanied by another dog who had doubtless been keeping her company all night. Do you know, Addey, the moment she saw me, away she bounded like a mad thing. I cannot imagine what could have possessed her. I missed two trains thinking she would come back again & I feel pretty sure she will do so & as soon as Tom secures her, he will forward her on to me & I'll take care she shall not have her liberty again for some time.

I am most sorry for this, Addey, and wish you to break the news to the Governor as gently as you can. She won't be lost, I know.

Love to all, dear Addey,
Ever yours,
George

I'll write again immediately when I hear of Eppie's welfare.

George leaves Devon with the dog Addey's father has given him, to go to Bristol to visit his family and then to return to London. Eppie had already shown signs of a rebellious nature and a definite lack of canine subservience. George's account of her giving him the slip is not out of character. Evidently she preferred a life of uncertain freedom to one of confinement in London. Addey postpones telling her father about this.

9 July 1850 Bowdon

My own dearest George,

Now that all is quiet for Father and Mother are gone to bed and I am alone waiting for Alicia who is in to town, I will commence answering your letter which I received this morning and glad was I to do so. I read it, love, with very mixed feelings of pleasure and disappointment, for I was much pleased to hear of your safe arrival, but very, very sorry to be informed of Eppie's disappearance. I do hope you will get her again. I did not say one word to Father about the loss for you may obtain possession of her again, and if not, it will always be soon enough to tell him about it.

You can't tell, dear, how much I miss you. I should hardly have thought it possible considering that you were here for so short a time. And so you really think I sometimes doubted your love for me? If such suspicions have ever crossed my mind, they have ever been but momentary for I have instantly crushed them as I would an insidious enemy. No, my love, I have full confidence in your affection, but I shall tell you, dearest, what I felt. That you have lost something of the *respect* you used to feel for me. I have been questioning myself as to the cause. Is it really as I fear, or does the change exist only in my imagination? I hope the latter for I would have *respect* as well as *love.* Can it be that our love will grow cold as we grow old? Once having loved, can we ever cease to love? It would be to surrender an attribute of the gods to give up the privilege of loving. Am I getting romantic? Well, then, I will say no more on that subject although I could run on all night nearly on the beauty of affection, but perhaps it is and will be best to let our *actions* speak for us.

We have sent on your pipe by a Lady so you must not be surprised if you receive a note from her. If she goes near Smithfield she will call on you with it herself, so if you see a rather tall Lady in black, you may expect her to give you a parcel and you may call her Mrs. Lovell. She is the same person who stopped the gig to ask you to side in to the station last Tuesday. And you may know her further to be the housekeeper at Bowdon. I have also sent you a pocket handkerchief which I hope you will like.

Alicia is not come yet and (it is past eleven) I have nothing else to do, so you may screw your courage to the sticking point, and pay particular attention to what I have to say. In the first place, I wish to be informed of the exact state of your health and spirits, and secondly, whether you have procured for yourself lodgings that please you?

Well, dearest, I dare say you are tired of all this crossing so I won't try your patience any longer.

Good bye my best, my darling George.

Ever your own
Addey

Have you heard any news of Eppie yet?

When Addey's father does learn of Eppie's loss, months later, he has his own response: "Ah, poor Addey! You will be obliged to be your own protection when he has got you. It will be vain to expect him to take care of you."

Mrs. Lovell, the "rather tall Lady in black" who has been asked to give George his pipe, is the housekeeper at Bowdon Manor. This is the only reference in the letters to Bowdon Lodge's much grander neighbor. They share a common driveway, with

Bowdon Lodge closer to the road. The day I visited, there was no sign of life at Bowdon Manor, which had become a photography museum and was closed.

11 July 1850

64 Bartholomew Close
Smithfield

Dearest Addey,

I have been out of town every day this week & nearly my usual day's work to do when I return so that I really am getting used up. Dear little soul, you have been wondering why I haven't written, I know, don't be cross love, will you. I'll write again as soon as I can get a spare half hour. When are you going to Cornwall? How is Mother? Jem Carter & myself are going to Cockfosters Sunday next. Shall I hear from you this week?

Goodbye dear,
ever yours,
Geo Virtue

Jem and Annie Glanville are quite well I believe.

16 July 1850

64 Bartholomew Close
Smithfield

My dearest Addey,

You are a good little soul for writing so soon. I hardly thought you would. You are too good for me, Addey. You may depend on it you are.

I used to fancy I liked warm weather but I am much inclined to alter my opinion now. Dear me, I think I have never felt the heat so oppressive as it is at present. I have the windows & door wide open, too, & my coat & waistcoat off & all to no purpose. How I should like to be at Bowdon now instead of in this dreadful old dirty nasty beastly city. There, I think I am a little cooler now.

Carter, Jem Glanville, & myself went to Cockfosters last Sunday & a glorious day we spent. We slept at Clampitts on the Saturday & started away at 7 am in a sort of dog cart, which Carter or Mr. Clampitt managed to procure from somewhere.

William & the Mrs. & the little ones are all quite well and jolly. They desire me to send their kind love to you all.

The Great Northern Railway will be opened in a few weeks & there will be a station close by your brother's house & I have no doubt his trade will be much increased thereby, & if you come up next summer won't it be jolly for me to be able to run down of a Saturday evening & back again on the next day. 'Twill be reminding us of days gone by, Addey love, won't it. Ah me! Those were happy times indeed (barring when I would miss a train or so). I suppose there are many more in store for us both yet. Oh, yes, I'm sure there are. That's the way to say it. Hurrah for the good times coming. Oh, when next you write to Mrs. Glanville please to tell her that her brother William is rather disappointed that he has not heard from her once since her marriage. My love to her also & is the busy time nearly over yet?!!!

I perfectly coincide with you Addey that picnics are nothing without ladies, & from the little experience I have had in these matters I am also inclined to think that when the number of ladies far exceed those of the other sex it places the gentlemen in a most trying and perplexing situation.

Our party were prevented from going to Hemmault Forest by the rain and not by *oversleeping* nor for want of determination to go if it had been fine. I don't think I shall give my word for another similar excursion more especially as Jem will not be one of the party.

That same Sunday Harris & I went to Gravesend and spent a tolerably miserable sort of day altogether.

Well, my dear Addey, I cannot write any more so goodbye. 'Tis awfully hot.

Love to all,
Yours ever,
Geo Virtue

Write soon.

I have enclosed a bit of (oh, I can't spell it). I found a bit of forget-me-not but Master Carter managed to steal it from me.

23 July 1850 — 64 Bartholomew Close, Smithfield

My dear little Addey,

And so you flatter my vanity by leaving me to infer why it is you prefer writing to me, before any other person. Oh you young turk! Wouldn't I pay you out for this if I was living a trifle nearer Bowdon. Upwards of 100 miles away – it seems a long distance to be apart, Addey dear, doesn't it. (My little canary is washing himself & spurting the water all over your letter so if you see any marks on it you may know what caused them. I wonder what it was ever so long ago that caused some blob to be on a letter I received from Miss Addey.)

That was a long parenthesis, dear, wasn't it, let me see what were we talking about. Oh, yes, the long distance we are from each other. Yes it is a long way indeed love, too far, a great deal. Do you know dear I get most awfully impatient & almost savage sometimes when I think it is next to impossible for me to see you for so *long* a time & if these are my feelings here what would they be if I went to 'Meriker!? No 'twon't do to go there at all, why I should never live through the passage.

I say, Addey, my son, I was disappointed because I wanted to send you down my miniature for a birthday gift but I couldn't you know. There is always some rascally tailor or other dun constantly sending me in their "little bills" just when I can least spare the cost. However, you know I *have begun* to be economical and I am *sure* I shall be a rich man *someday*. If I live, & Addey loves me, there's a good time coming.

Why does Father say you shall not come to London next summer?

How is Mother? & Alicia? Give my love to 'em all & to your cousins. Which of all your cozes should you think I love best, Addey? You can't guess, I know, nor I won't tell you if you cannot.

Quarter to six. Time to leave off, so goodbye darling.

Write soon to your own,
George

30 July 1850

64 Bartholomew Close
London

My dearest Addey,

How are you this morning & how is Alicia & Mother & Father? All quite well, I hope.

And Mrs. Glanville is still happy as ever, well I can scarcely see how she can be otherwise & you envy her! Do you? Oh very well Miss, suppose I said I envied Tom what would you say to that – kick up a jolly row, I'm bound – but I don't envy him a bit in the world. I only wish little Addey & I were Mr. & Mrs. Virtue, that's all.

Sometimes I wonder if I shall ever be able to keep a wife & a house & all that sort of thing. I think I should be a very proud fellow then, no mistake. Only fancy leaving this dull miserable place of an evening & having to trot home to a nice little cottage & little Addey (as Mrs. GLV, of course) inside waiting, all smiles and good nature. But it's quite impossible for me to describe what happy thoughts of this nature I often very often indulge in. What do you think about it, Addey, eh? Now don't you think I shall make a good husband, oh yes, I'm sure I would. I should be so attentive & come home every night quite early (I think it a most cruel practice for husbands to keep their dear little wives waiting up for them) & I wouldn't smoke. At least no I shouldn't want to smoke I'm sure. Not unless you were cross & kicked up a row, but you are too good tempered for that, love. Oh, I quite think we should be a very happy couple. Well I shall save up & buy some furniture & get married at once. Hurrah! We shouldn't want a very extensive establishment at first you know. I'm sure if I had little Addey for my wife I should get on better. Sometimes I am very foolish and extravagant. Now if I had little Addey to look after me a bit why she would be able to tell me if I were doing wrong & advise me & talk kindly to me. How I love you, Addey, you are so kind & good, always the same. I have seen you pretend to be out of temper now & then but I knew perfectly well at the time it was all sham. I always think you are the least cross when you try to be so. Well dear I must go now. I had a long dream about you last night.

Goodbye love. Write to me soon.

Your Affectionate Husband
(that sounds rather grand),
George Virtue

You don't love as fervently as I do, Addey. Yes you do, kiss me.

I am going on Hampstead Heath on Thursday morning at 5 am to see the sun rise. I shall sleep in Camden Town the night previously. Old brother Bill is in Wales. Would you like to write to him? Here's his address. W.D. Virtue at Mr. Wells', Commercial Road, Newport, Monmouth.

He has been unsteady & he is lonely now. I'm sure it would do him good if you wrote to him. I think Father will come down with me next summer. No news of Eppie yet. I'm afraid the Governor will think *me* a poor protector. Should you have more faith, love?

George paints an appealing picture of married life with Addey, once again affirming her good influence on him. Did this continue through their married life? I hope it did and they were happy. I suspect they were.

9 August 1850 Bowdon

My dearest George,

I am very cross, so I shall not write a long letter. I think I was stupid to have given you the aforesaid very interesting piece of information. I ought to have allowed you to have discovered that same by the light of thine own understanding. Nevertheless, it is said and cannot be unsaid. I don't know that I have any reason for being so miserable but I am unreasonable sometimes you know, don't you? Perhaps it is that I haven't slept long enough. Perhaps it is, but I can't tell why, I can't even guess why it is. Now I know if you were here you would tell me it is very wrong, and very foolish, and I ought to know better. For I will say that for you, really you always tell me of my faults when they come under your notice and I love you all the more for it. You are a dear fellow! I wish you would think I don't care anything about you and I don't because then I could teaze you and make you feel rather perplexed, you know.

So you didn't even *go* to see the sun rise. Oh George, I wish, I do wish you wouldn't say things which you don't mean, make promises you never intend to fulfil and all these very amusing little pleasantries, no doubt surely very wrong. I think this sort of thing is almost your greatest fault. You promise *without thinking* and then when the time comes for its fulfillment you find yourself prevented either by your inclination or something of more importance. You know this is *true* dear, *and wrong.* A man should ever keep his word or he loses reliance and *honor.* For of what value is the honor of a man whose word is not to be trusted? Even in his own eyes? Surely but of *very* little. George you *must* break yourself of this habit of promising without thinking, indeed you must, love, for your own sake and it is very wrong saying that which we do not mean on *any subject*, for it gives one a wrong idea of character which is not to be desired in *you.* Forgive me my dear George for saying that much, but these remarks in themselves must show you how much I have your interest at heart. I know you are not angry with me or I shouldn't write so freely on a rather unpleasant theme as the contemplation on others' faults, especially *yours* must ever be, but then no one is perfect.

How did you and your cousin get on with your second swimming match? Who won? I think I'll bet on – not on *you*, but on Mr. James.

I dare say your uncle thinks you are a dreadful young man writing to young ladies about lodgings. Oh dear me how I should have liked to have been you when he was talking to you about it. How annoyed you looked! I can quite fancy the expression on your face and then to think that he wouldn't be convinced! Oh horrible, most horrible!

Well, I said I shouldn't write a long letter and I won't write any more, so addio.

Yours etc.,
Addey

Mother is rather better, but still poorly. Sends her love. Also Alicia. N.B. I didn't say all that about your not keeping your word, because you didn't go to see the sun rise entirely, but because it is a *general failing.*

Addey's remark about George not hesitating to mention her faults is puzzling. (I can't remember his citing a single instance.) She then launches into a lecture, suggesting he could do better on following through on promises. George takes this all in stride.

Empty envelope from George to Addey, postmarked 13 August 1850

August 18 Bowdon

My dearest George,

I was delighted to find from your letter that you were not displeased with me. Not that I expected you would be, for I am well pleased to say I know you better. You half promise therein to make no more promises, keep it, dear. It will be a great good gained, which will make me very happy to know I have been in some sort the means of accomplishing. It will only require a little *forethought* on your part, love. Did I say you make promises without *intending* to keep them? No, I did not mean that for I do not believe you *ever* did that. Yet, if promises are frequently broken one may be apt to think so. But *I know* you never do that.

I am very much obliged for the paper and like it very much. We have never seen any of them before, and if all the rest of the numbers are as interesting as this one I shall like it exceedingly. Your taste in the choice of literature is always good.

And you want to make me believe you are a very faulty animal, do you? Well and so I do. But you have not so many as you say you have. I know what it is, you only say all this that I may discover when I *am* with you always, how you have libeled yourself. Will you tell me, love, why your landlady said your name should be Vice instead of Virtue?

Now my love I must make haste and conclude. Tom is just come over from Torquay for a few hours only, so you know I must not pay him such a bad compliment as to be writing much while he is here. Our little Alicia is very ill, poor little thing.

So you did lose at the grand swimming match. Well I think your good cousin deserves a high compliment from me for enabling me to win my bet, and as for you, you are the best fellow in all the world for losing it. Well you are a darling.

And "with all thy faults I love thee still."

Goodbye my dearest,
Your own Addey

20 August 1850 — 64 Bartholomew Close, London

My dear Addey,

I have just time to say how d'ye do and goodbye for an old fellow has been in here bothering me all the afternoon when I wanted to be writing to little Addey. Hang him. Never mind, love, you shall have a good long letter next week.

I have had the influenza for the last two or three days but I am nearly quite well of it now, thank you.

Bill sends his love to you & to *Winnie* when you write again.

Goodbye dear. Write soon to your loving,

George

Kind love to all. Mother is nearly well by this time I hope. I hope you will enjoy yourself at Torquay Regatta.

29 August 1850 — 64 Bartholomew Close, London

My dear little Addey,

Well how have you passed your time at Torquay? I presume you are returned & that's why I direct the letter as usual to Bowdon. Did you expect I should write to you while you were at Torquay, love? Yes, I think you did & I scarcely know now what prevented me. For one reason I have been very busy all the week.

My influenza, cold, or what you please to call it is not quite well yet, tho I am much better this afternoon. I have gone straight home every night this week, Addey. There, how steady I am to be sure.

Mr. & Mrs. Clampitt are returned home & as I feel somewhat better today I think I will go down & see them both this evening.

I called at Jem Glanville's on Sunday evening. They are both well (I mean Annie & Jem – Annie for the second time requested me to ask you when she might expect the pleasure of receiving an answer to her last letter to you. I can't make out you two girls at all. You appear quite friendly & write each other most loving epistles & yet I do believe you are not good friends at heart. What is it?)

Oh, I was nearly forgetting that you expect me to blow up a bit for your not writing me sooner the last time but as I don't feel in good humour for doing so now, if you please, I'll wait till another time.

Did you see Bess Godfrey at Torquay? I understand she is coming to London en route to Paris.

Is Mother better?

I went to Reading on Sunday week. I was on the lookout for poor little Eppie nearly the whole day but I could see nothing of her. Tom Mullen's private opinion is that "she has walked clean out of the world."

Goodbye, Addey dear. I don't at all expect or wish to receive a letter from you on Saturday (because you will be tired no doubt), but write as soon as you can, like a good girl. Kind love to all.

Yours affectionately,
Geo L. Virtue

I think if I had little Addey to nurse me I should often want to be ill on purpose – dear little soul – give us a kiss.

23 September 1850 64 Bartholomew Close

My dear little Addey,

Now, if you did but know how truly unhappy I have been ever since I sent you that foolish & unkind letter. (I'm glad you sent it back to me, for I have burnt it; & I wish I could as easily efface its contents from your memory.) I know your kind heart would be half-inclined to forgive me. I wrote it in haste, Addey dear, & under a strong fit of jealousy, presuming that you did not care at all about me & that you were wishing to break off our correspondence altogether. I as firmly believe now I was mistaken as I *then* felt prejudiced against you. In fact, your kind letter of this morning – the latter part of it, particularly – quite reassured me of your strong & unbiased attachment. Bless you, my own dear Addey. Can you forgive me for being so cruel & unfeeling?

I wish you had not said anything to Alicia about it. She has put a cold & quite incorrect construction on the contents of my note. How glad I am, Addey, that you *know* my heart too well to give credit to her idea & yet I think you half doubt at times whether I really love you or not. I love you most sincerely, Addey, quite as strongly as ever – but it is a fierce kind of love sometimes, Addey, which makes me feel quite wretched. I wish I could always be cool & happy as I feel now, for it is only in such moments as these that I feel the holy, pure blessedness of your love. It is only when I fancy (without reason, I confess) you do not care for me that I feel wicked & savage – more like a wild beast than a man. You are the only being in the world who produces this effect in my mind, but know this, Addey, if ever my feelings are worked up to such a pitch again (which God forbid), a few *kind* words from you would bring me back to my proper senses – instantly.

What first excited me was the fact of your having so many enemies in Torquay (I hate the place) & yet your going as it were right into the heart of them & remaining there so long. I could not prevent myself from believing that some powerful attraction kept you there. Even at the present moment I can scarcely refrain from feeling a slight pang of jealousy although I place full & implicit confidence in your love for me.

Try & forget the contents of my last letter, love, & forgive me as soon as you can.

Will you write to me again this week?

Ever yours,
Geo. L. Virtue

Once again letters from Torquay cause problems.

1 October 1850 — 64 Bartholomew Close

My dear Addey,

I have but a few minutes to spare you – I have been extremely busy all day "stock taking," a most tedious, dirty, & uncomfortable piece of work it is too, I assure you, & I am not at all sorry I have nearly finished my job.

I thought you were too good & kind to bear malice, bless your heart. But I say, Addey, you don't show *all* my letters, do you? Because I must be careful what I say in the future if you do.

Poor Mother, I am extremely sorry to hear she is no better. We must always hope for the best. I trust she is not so seriously ill as you have been led to imagine.

Give my kind love to her, please.

I went down to Bristol the other Sunday & saw Father & Ted & Tom. Bill is in Wales not doing much good for himself, I'm afraid. Brother Jim obtained his discharge from the Fusiliers as far back as February last & 10 pounds was forwarded to him to pay his passage back to England. Strange to say he has not written to any one of us since nor have we yet been able to learn what is become of him.

I can't stay to write any more so goodbye.

Yours Affectionately,
Geo Little Virtue

Any news from India?

9 October 1850 Bowdon

My dearest George,

The sun is shining gloriously, and the dewdrops hanging on the leaves look like nothing so much as diamonds. There is an old rook – what you would call a *crow* – on the oak tree opposite, cawing like an old friend, almost making one think 'tis bright spring time, but then alas! the "sere and yellow leaf" quickly dispel that pleasant fancy: and yet I know not why it should be more pleasant to fancy it spring than autumn, for now we have the long winter evenings to anticipate, and what's so delightful as a quiet winter fireside at home? You see I am beginning to like quiet again, yes I am rapidly settling down to my old love of home.

I wish you were here for I am just now in a gossiping good humour. Oh George, my love! How did you enjoy yourself at Clampitt's on Tuesday night? I should have liked to have it in my power to make myself invisible and then to have joined the party. Were there many ladies there? Who were they, and who did you flirt with? You must tell me all about it, you know. Oh, you are a terrible boy, I dare say you did. Never mind, I shall serve you out when you come down again. I owe you a lot, only you must stay longer than you did last time.

How I should like to have been at Cockfosters the other day when you called. How you would have stared to have seen me. You would not have believed the evidence of your own blessed pair of eyes, would you? It would be such a pleasure to take you by surprise. Only fancy one evening when you are at home quietly sipping your tea, to have a card placed in your hand with "Miss Adelaide Watson" on it. Why you would drop your teacup and I'm not sure you wouldn't drop yourself, too, in your extreme fright. Oh! dear me yes. Certainly that pleasure is reserved for me, sometime to be realized, so remember whenever I come to London, I shall be very secret about it.

So you really have not much time to spare, have you? Well then, dearest, I won't be unreasonable, but then you *promised* me a long letter *sometimes*. It was so long ago that I feared you had forgotten that same promise. Had you?

Well, I think it's rather cold now although it's sunny. I wonder if it be colder in town. By the way, is your scarf worn out? And do you want another? If you tell me what color, I shall knit it. Do you remember the first time I put on the last to you? I do – as if it were but yesterday. What a long time ago it was! Alas, alas, how time flies! Ah well, I am glad of it, for soon winter will be gone and spring just following, and then you will be here again, my own darling George.

Mother is a little better and has changed her mind again about going to Plymouth. She desires her love be sent to you.

Good bye my dearest, believe me

Ever yours only,
Addey

After the tumult of the previous month, their correspondence has returned to its usual tenor. George's teasing is shown by his facetious response to Addey's light-hearted query on whether he flirted with the ladies. George surely did have an eye for the ladies, but his heart belonged to Addey.

15 October 1850 — 64 Bartholomew Close

My dearest Addey,

Thank you, love, for sending your last letter a day before I expected it. It was a joyful surprise indeed. Only I felt as if I wanted another the next day, but that would have been too covetous, wouldn't it? I wanted to write yesterday, but I was prevented from doing so, nor shall I be able to send a very long one this time, as I had to escort my sister and cousin Betsy down to Uncle Lenny's for tea.

Bless your heart, as you know your image has been in my mind *constantly* ever since Friday morning. It is only after I feel I have been unkind to you that my true & devoted love for you kindles up again almost to too great a pitch, for I fill my head up with all sorts of romantic ideas, that for a time take away all my thoughts from business matters.

I didn't *flirt much* at Mr. Clampitts the other evening. I only kissed the ladies all round twice.

I was rather unwell last week but I laid by on Sunday & took a blue pill & now I'm quite lively & jolly again, hurrah!

I should like you to make another scarf, if you please. The choice of colours I leave to you as your taste is better. The last was a very neat & serviceable one.

Do you know when I go out I cannot help frequently eyeing some pretty little figure which in my fancy I mistake for Addey – but when I get near enough, I, of course, perceive my mistake.

Give my love to Mother (who I hope is still improving) & Alicia & the Governor & accept the same with no end of kisses from

Yours ever,
Affectionately,
Geo Virtue

18 October 1850

My own dear George,

I would be able to write to you a longer letter tomorrow but I know, dearest, you will be expecting to hear before then, are you not, love?

You are often unwell. I fear you do not take sufficient care of yourself. If you don't, I will be very, very angry indeed. Seriously, you know you ought now winter is coming again, and you must take care of yourself for *my* sake (for I do care a little bit about you, I think) if not for your own. Mother, I am happy to report, still continues to get better. I hope now she will soon be well. She talks of going to London in the spring but she has *talked* of doing so for so long a time, that I don't think it very likely she will do so. Neither do I think she will be well enough.

Have you heard from Jim yet? I am very anxious about him. Somehow I feel a particular interest in him. I wish he were home.

So you confess you flirted a little the other evening at Mr. Clampitt's? Very well, Sir! I shall serve you out for all this when I see you. You may depend upon it!

By the way, how do your *whiskers* grow? Because I'm thinking I may be able to *pull* them occasionally. Do you think it will be possible? Because I wouldn't indulge in such anticipations if you don't, for I don't at all like to be disappointed, you know. I should like to try them now and satisfy myself as to their capabilities. I think you had better send me down a hair or two (*if you can spare them*) that I may be myself some sort of judge.

You won't be displeased at the short affair, will you, dearest? Nor doubt the truth of

Your own little Addey

➺ *Quite an intimate request from Addey. Of course she was unaware that her words would be read some 170 years after they were written by a curious descendant.*

29 October 1850 — 64 Bartholomew Close

My dearest Addey,

What a good girl you are to be sure & don't I love you better & better every day. I think you will make a capital little wife, Addey, & I would try all in my power to make you happy & comfortable. You are not very difficult to please so this would not be a very difficult task.

I should like to see you in this neat little bonnet. I'm bound you look very pretty. Now, I like for you to tell all these little affairs of yours, so don't you say any more about bothering me because 'tis no such thing. I'm delighted indeed to learn you enjoy such good health. Take regular exercise in the morning air every day, Addey. You will be the better for it. Fancy I'm with you. You used to like walking with me, love, didn't you? Well, I shall be with you in spirit. You are always uppermost in my thoughts, you little darling rascal. I wish I could kiss you, that's all.

Lawrence was taken seriously ill Friday night & poor Harriet was telegraphed for to come down to him immediately. She went down at once & found him insensible. He still remains in a very precarious state. I trust he will recover, poor fellow. His loss would prove a most serious & distressing thing to his poor wife & children.

I went to the War Office about Jim yesterday but I could not then learn anything of him. I must call again this week. I hardly think he would go anywhere else without writing to say so & yet this is the most favourable light to account for his non-appearance.

Good bye, my own dear Addey,
Ever yours constantly,
Geo Virtue

Love to Mother (does she improve still?) & Alicia & the Governor. An improvement in folding, I think. Thank you.

Lawrence is George's brother-in-law, his sister Harriet's husband. George stayed with them in Camden Town before he found accommodations in Bartholomew Close, Smithfield, in London.

1 NOVEMBER 1850 BOWDON

My dearest George,

How has this year passed with you? Rapidly? To me it has flown more swiftly than I can understand. I wonder why it is that sometimes time flies so rapidly and at other times it lags as if it would never pass? I do not think it can or does always depend on the state of our feelings, for I don't think I have been *particularly* happy this summer and yet it has flown like a dream. What can be the reason, then?

I was dreaming about you all last night. Not that you were here, but that I was in town and was teaching you to play at cribbage! and didn't know myself, but you were obstinate and *would* have it your own way which was wrong! Just like you, you know. Oh you are such a naughty boy! – And such a darling! And you think I will be easily pleased, do you? I am very difficult to please, I can tell you. I am very fastidious. Do you remember my telling you so a long time ago, in the first days of our acquaintance. What a compliment I paid you then! But you were too modest to see it or pretended not to, but you are a love and the very best fellow in all the world. There's no doubt about that, at least in my estimation.

And the better I know you, dearest, the more I love you and will it be ever thus? I hope so, I think so – if it be possible, we shall be very happy. What would life be without love? A dull matter. Those who love truly, what can they not bear. We are and shall be blessed!

Have you heard from your sister? How is she and Mr. Lawrence? Is he better? I hope with her care he may recover for the power of love is great.

I hope your fears will not be realized about Jim. For myself, I have great hopes.

Mother still improves slowly. All else are well. We had a letter from Winnie on Sunday who is also well and sends her love to you. So do the rest.

Good bye, dearest,
Your love,
Addey

5 November 1850 64 Bartholomew Close

My own dear little Addey,

Only a few words this time, my dear. I am busy today, really.

Those were very pretty sentiments in your last letter & in the sense of them I perfectly coincide with yourself, but my time now is generally so much taken up that I very seldom have time to reflect on how rapidly time is fleeting away.

Sunday evening I *went to church* & I saw there such a pretty little girl. She was in the body of the church & I was in the gallery, but I was much struck by the forcible resemblance she bore to yourself, but it then was gaslight. Perhaps she will not look so well by day. Shall I go next Sunday & see?

I long to be with you again, dear Addey, & I think I miss you more now than ever. Dear little Addey, I love you extremely. When you are my wife how proud & happy I shall be. I have written this nearly in the dark so excuse the scrawling & expect a longer letter next time,

From yours ever,
Affectionately,
Geo L. Virtue

Lawrence improves. No news from Jim yet.

When we are married, Addey, if you like we will have a pew at Christ's Church. I like the place much & it is quite near here. I think I'm getting religious.

15 November 1850 64 Bartholomew Close

My dear little Addey,

How are you this fine afternoon? It isn't at all like November weather here – the days are quite sunshiney & mild.

The Lord Mayor's show was considered a very grand affair by the Cockneys principally – for myself I don't think much of it. I saw the procession go by St. Paul's & was nearly suffocated by two stout old ladies in the crowd for my pains. So you were up here four years ago. Then I was in Devonshire. What a changing world. Four years ago, it seems a long time back. Who did you like best in the world then Addey, or did you care for anybody? You do care a little about me, dear, don't you? & don't I love you for it.

Oh yes, I went to church on Sunday morning, but not *purposely* to see the pretty girl. *I went to hear the sermon* because I like the preacher & then I wanted to tell you how this pretty girl looked by daylight as you asked me to. Well, she is pretty, Addey, & like you, too – somewhat, but I was very intent on the sermon & so I couldn't spare very much time to look at her & I was thinking of you nearly all the time. Do you go to church every Sunday? Because if you don't, you have no right to blow me up for non-attending. Of course, my dear, when you are my wife (my dear little wife Addey) I shall always be most proud & happy to take you to church or anywhere else you please & I shall be so attentive to you, dear, I'm sure I shall have neither time nor inclination to look at pretty girls at all, be they ever so pretty. What is all the world to me without my darling Addey, bless her heart.

Sunday night I had to go to Ipswich on business & I returned late last night. All the way coming home I was picturing to myself how jolly it would be if little Addey were at home at 64 Bartholomew Close amorously waiting for my return & how glad & smiling she would be to see me home safe – instead of going to my solitary lodgings with no one to see or care about me, all lonely.

Good bye, Addey dear, tis dark & I can't see to write any more.

Love to all,
Yours ever, Geo L Virtue

I shall come down next summer if possible, dear.

5 December 1850 Bowdon

My dearest George,

Another week gone and Thursday evening again! What glorious weather, positively. The flowers mistaking the season are beginning to bud and even bloom. Strange that it should be so mild now in December. Father said yesterday that it was hot enough for midsummer. We can sit on the porch as we do in the summer, without feeling at all cold.

You will be sorry to hear that our cousin Carrie is very unwell indeed. We expected her up today but I fear she is not well enough to venture out. She talks of going to Torquay in a week or two, and much wishes me to accompany her. Shall I? I confess I am afraid to do so, for the place is dreadfully unlucky for me, and you, I know, would rather for me to remain where I am – although *perhaps* you won't say so. However, I believe you may rest easy for I do not think I will go.

And you really think you would be "forlorn" if you had not your little Addey to think about you, but if you had not little Addey, you would have a little somebody else. But I don't like to think of another's supplanting me in your love. No, dear, it must not be! I shall still hold the place I have, and still be your little Addey. You don't know, dearest, how proud I am of your love, and how happy it makes me. How lucky it was that I went to that delightful Ball! some three years ago! What a long time!

I won't be able to help loving you, I fear! I should like to see you. I wish summer would come! We shall meet with greater confidence in each other next year, love, than we felt last, do you not think so?

I am knitting a pair of mittens for a certain gentleman. I shall not tell you who he is. Either I knit very slowly or there is a great deal of work in them, so they take some time doing or he would have had them before now. I think I have a mania for knitting for verily I have not done so much before.

Mother and Alicia send their love to you.

Yours ever,
Addey Watson

Have you heard anything of Jim yet?
I am to have a long letter next time. Remember, dearest?

19 December 1850 Bowdon

My dearest George,

Oh it is such a glorious night! The moon is full and it is clear, not a cloud. I quite long for a walk only 'tis cold and rather dirty. If I had a companion I think I would dare the mud for the sake of the moonlight. As I have not (for Alicia won't go) I shall stay at home and write to you.

I was so surprised to hear of your father's wedding. Do you know the bride? I hope they will be very happy. If you do not know her, are you not very curious to see her?

By the way, George, how are you, dearest? You said you stayed in the house all Sunday, that you had a bad cold, but you did not say you were better. Are you? I wish you were going to spend your Christmas with us. Where will you be? You must tell me if it be merry or not.

Thanks love for your last letter. It is positively a treat to get a letter from you in which you say much of *yourself.* You can never say too much or indeed *enough* of yourself to satisfy your little Addey. *Remember that.*

Have I told you Lizzie is in Salisbury? In a shop, she likes it much. She is very well and has a lover, and above all, is very happy. I wonder if this be a natural consequence. I don't know, never having been unhappy, at least for any considerable time. Do you know I think I have a careless sort of disposition, passing off sorrows lightly. I trust I shall never be tried with any very bitter trouble.

My love, what a strange idea of yours to desire to have my letters buried with you when you die. What a terrible thought. Surely the earth without you would be dark, an impenetrable darkness! You should not talk of it to me, my love. I must not even dream of such a thing.

You requested me to send a long letter this time but I fear me I cannot. Frank is waiting and he is very curious to know if "Mr. George is coming down at Christmas." I wish he was, but patience!

The sun is shining oh most gloriously, the sky is a beautiful bright pale almost pearly blue. Oh, I so wish you were here to admire its purity with me. You don't see such skies in London. Well, never mind, when we live in the country you know you will. Meantime I am as much yours as then I shall be. Good bye, my love,

Your own
Addey

Alas, George's prior letter stating his wish that Addey's letters be buried with him is not among those which survived. Perhaps this odd wish of his emanated partially from his loneliness in London. George is a romantic. It is strange for me to think of their having this dialogue so long ago. I feel that they are in some way still here. The impermeable curtain between our living and dying is a conundrum of the first order.

23 December 1850 — 64 Bartholomew Close

My dear little Addey,

It is just breathing time with me so I embrace the opportunity of writing to you, my dear, because tomorrow I expect to be very busy all day.

It was a very natural idea of Master Frank's to wish to know if I was coming down this Xmas & I only wish I could answer yes. I should like to come down very much, but as I cannot, 'tis no use fretting. We have never spent Christmas Day together, Addey – but I hope we shall & many of them.

So you don't like to think about my dying. Do you know, I was thinking this over in my mind this morning at four o'clock. (I slept at my sister's last night & I never sleep very soundly there.) I concluded that you must *learn to think* of this *for it is certain.* I have seen & thought so much on this subject since I've been in London that I can contemplate it quite composedly. In fact, I rather like to think there will be an end sometime & then I try to think beyond death & then I get lost, but what nonsense this is, my dear (I think I'm rather mad at times). I hope I'm not going to die for many years to come.

For Addey's sake I would live forever & and we will, dear. Our loves shall be always – for ever.

Frank is returned from school & Harriet from Bristol. She gives a most flattering description of "Mother." So good, so kind & amiable – about 38 – rather tall, stout, and good-looking – nice teeth – a very pretty mouth – & a sort of rural simplicity about her manner which makes her altogether quite loving & lovable. I really quite wish to see my stepmother.

Little Frank, of course, is a great fellow now, full of anecdotes about his schoolmates & he tries to bother his uncle with very fierce & awful Latin conjugations.

Tell me a long story, dear, in your next of how you have spent your Christmas.

Believe me I shall be with you in spirit all Xmas though we are so many miles apart. Tomorrow evening (as last year) we have a turn off of beef & beer at Ivey Lane for all hands (barring the Governor). Then we propose health & make speeches & some of the juveniles get very dreadful & so winds up Xmas Eve. On the Xmas Day I am invited to dine at Finsbury Square where we have a very grand dinner on a large scale. Then, lots of pianoing & squalling – oh no, that isn't the thing at all, *singing, of course,* & quadrilles & my cousin Frances *honours* me *so much* as to polka with me in preference to anyone else – because I'm a cousin – & it would be slightly immoral, I suppose, or *not pious* to polka with anyone stranger. On the 26th I'm going down to Reading to shoot blackbirds & drink gin & water with Tom Mullen & so will terminate *my* Xmas festivities.

Yes, I ought to leave off smoking. (I think I made a rather premature & inconsiderate promise on this topic once before, did I?) Well, my dear, I most solemnly declare if my leaving it off will conduce to your happiness I most certainly will. When we are married I only *intend* to smoke when you put my pipe out, are cross, or won't get up to go out for a walk in the morning with me, dear little soul. I know you would spoil me by indulging me too much.

Now I can't write any more so won't bother.

Good bye,
Always,
GV

My cold is quite gone now, thank you, and I am pretty jolly. How are you & how is the headache? Your pearly blue sky at Bowdon & this nice thick fog here the morning form a striking contrast.

Love to all

I like the description of George's new stepmother, with the distinctive name of Hannah Mountain, as having a "rural simplicity." She had courage marrying into a family of six sons and one daughter. She and George's father would have another daughter, Frances.

Destiny of the Letters

The actual destiny of the letters would have been beyond George's wildest imaginings. First, that they did survive, or many of them did, and by some miracle, they endured for more than a century and a half, crossed the Atlantic Ocean three times, and came into the hands of their direct descendants, who would read them in a world far removed from the one in which they were written.

Many of the letters were saved by both Addey and George – except for the truly hurtful ones from George, which he tells us he burned. After they were wed, they must have kept the letters with them when they lived in New York and Boston and then, finally, in Toronto.

George and Addey's daughter Harriet Louisa, known to the family as Aunt Louie, must have taken the letters with her to England after her mother's death. She led a peripatetic existence there, visiting relatives for most of her adult life, supported by her brothers, who were directed by their mother to do so. Mary Fillingham's son, Tony, told me he remembered Aunt Louie fondly as being lots of fun, very pretty, and playing games with him when she came to visit when he was a young boy in Topsham.

THURSDAY EVENING BOWDON

My dearest George,

I suppose you are now enjoying yourself with your friend Tom Mullen. A nice fellow I think he is. I have a sort of liking for him already. I think I shall like him when I know him for I *shall* know him, you know, someday – and his little wife, too. How much I should like to be able to peep in upon you. I daresay you are enjoying yourself.

My Christmas has been a particularly quiet one, and is like to continue so. I have been nowhere, am not going, and nobody has been here. Yesterday I went to church to hear the singing and splendid it was. They are getting a good choir again. They sang three magnificent anthems but truth to say, I was thinking more of my own beloved George than of the sermon.

And would you really, dearest, leave off smoking for me? You don't know how gratified I felt for the promise, and if I took you at your word, it would be for your sake partly for I feel convinced it is injurious to the constitution. I am hesitating even now to decide. No, love, I won't ask you to give it up *altogether,* only you shall promise to smoke only *very moderately.*

And you think I shall be cross sometimes when we are married, do you? Well, I am glad you do, for I dare say I shall. Tell me, George, are you ever cross? I never saw you so.

I *cannot* learn to think of your dying, dearest. I know it must be sometime, but oh I pray it may be very, very distant. I dare not think of it else. Every day my love grows stronger. Constantly am I finding something more to admire and to love. I do not say this to please you but because I feel it is so. Can it be possible that love such as ours can die with our youth? Shall we outlive its influence? No, it cannot, must not, shall not be! We shall love forever as you so hopefully and cheeringly say it shall always be, my beloved.

I am delighted that you have such a good stepmother. She must be such a nice body.

By the way what sport had you blackbird shooting? Mother wished you might not in mistake shoot yourself which Alicia thought was hardly likely seeing that you are more like a greybird or canary, she says. Alicia is very complimentary, sometimes. I am now going to bed.

I daresay you are singing. Have you been "sparring" today? Good bye,

Your Addey

We were invited to a party at Dartington on Xmas Day, but Father & Mother wouldn't let us go because they would be lonely.

George and Addey's Christmases were in sharp contrast. The description of George's sounds Dickensian: the feast at the senior George Virtue's establishment in Finsbury Square sounds very grand, indeed, with lavish food, singing, and dancing. His cousin Frances picked young George to polka with. I doubt if her choice of him as a dancing partner was based purely on their being cousins.

And on Boxing Day, our hero shoots blackbirds with his friend Tom Mullen (George's sidekick in the loss of Eppie), followed by a libation of gin and water.

Addey describes a quiet day, attending church, with a favorable comment on the choir. Both of them lament their never having spent the day together, something they hope for in the years ahead.

1851

A dreadful fancy man you are

1851 is the fourth year of the courtship and the last year George is in London.

The first letter of the year is from Addey.

9 JANUARY 1851 BOWDON

My dear George,

You think I shall make a "spoilt child" of you, do you? Well, I have no wish to do so I assure you for I have a strong dislike to all such beings, small or large.

Dear me, why *do* you begin sentences and leave them unfinished? Raising my curiosity so and setting me considering what you were going to say when you ended. Do you remember having done so? In your last note you have done so twice. One I can very well guess at its conclusion, but for the other I am divided on my choice. You begin by fearing that I shall kill you by kindness "when we are married" and then you say "but then, just never mind." Now *what do* you mean? Some say that when young ladies marry, they care not so much to please their husbands as when they were just lovers. Is that what you mean? Oh! I wish you were here! How I would teaze you. Never mind, I won't forget it when you *do* come. I think I owe you a lot of teazing, and you shall have it, I promise you.

And you really want to know why I was curious about your employment last Wednesday evening? Well, I won't satisfy you, but I do wish you did not remain in that old office so late, making up accounts. I won't allow it when I am near you. I wonder if I shall be able to help you. Do you think it likely? I do. I don't see why not.

Summer is coming very rapidly. I do hope we shall not have much stormy weather. Now the trees are beginning to bud again. Already some things are quite green. It will be a pity if they get cut back again. It is so mild and the days are getting longer. I shall be so glad for you will be here – not that I care anything at all about you!

What do you think, dear? Compton talks of coming home this year. Alicia can hardly tell whether he is only joking or if he really means it. I hope he does – and yet I hope he may not, for what we should do without Alicia I do not know (for I suppose he will take her away from us when he does come). Don't you think she has been constant? They have been engaged for nearly *twelve years!!* Dreadful! I never could endure it. But then I was going to say, if Spencer does come home this year I shall go to London most likely.

Shall I tell you what Father said when he knew of poor little Eppie's loss. (He does not know *when* she was lost, or *how*.) "Why," he said, after having expressed his regret and all that, "Ah, poor Addey! You will be obliged to be your own protection when he has got you. It will be vain to expect him to take care of you." There – what think you of that?

I know not if you will be able to find out the consecutive pages of my very excellent epistle. I confess it puzzled me. You see if I had not been thinking so much of you, I should not have blundered so – perhaps. Well, goodnight. 'Tis nearly bed time. You are a dreadful boy, you take away all my thoughts. I wish I could in the person say goodnight to you, but since I can only do so in the spirit, then, my love, good night. God bless you.

And continue to love,
Your little Addey

Does Addey share her father's doubts about George's ability to take care of her? It wouldn't be surprising if she did.

THURSDAY EVENING (MARCH) BOWDON

My dearest George,

You have no idea how quiet it is here. Both Father and Mother are reading and Alicia is gone, so you see I could do no better than put away my book, for I have been reading too, and silently talk to you – though not as we used to do by pointing to letters of the alphabet. Do you remember those evenings? Interesting employment, at least it used to be for me.

Alicia is gone to Hampstead. I very much wished to go but could not be permitted to venture outside the door, so precious am I! What a dreadful state of existence must be that of a confirmed invalid.

How wonderful it seems to me the time speeds away, nearly one year since you were here.

Sometimes I can hardly believe it. *Everything* lies so vividly before me that it appears as if it were only last month you went away. And if it passes so rapidly *now* what will it do when you come? Oh! It will fly like the mist before the sun.

There! I've snuffed out the candle again! Do you know what we say when a young lady commits such folly? Well, I've done it at least a dozen times this year! Oh dear, what shall I do?

> *Addey is referring to a folk belief that if you snuff out a candle, you will be married within the year. A candle snuffer was a scissors-like tool used to trim the wick.*

I received a letter today from a friend, one unknown to you. She is a lady and *such* a lady! I shall do you the honor of introducing you to her one day though you must promise first to be proof against her charms. She has flashing black eyes, sparkling wit, a ringing laugh and she is so pretty, a brunette, very merry, and good tempered, a heart to love – but I don't want *you* to fall in love with her.

So you like sunshine better than rain, do you? So do I. And I am associated in your mind with summer and sunshine, bright, glowing, glorious summer! I am glad of that – may I ever be so. You need not have cautioned me against contradicting your idea of my perfection because you know I most cordially agree with you.

Lizzy Taylor came to see me on Monday. She has an admirer, and when I asked his name, she said, "George. I'm determined to have a George, you know." There, I think it was *you* who made her adopt that resolution.

Do you remember the Misses Darnford at Torquay? Those two ladies who used to dress so oddly? Well, poor things, some time since their mother died and they were left entirely unprovided for, and greatly in debt. They went to Bath or Plymouth, I don't know which, where report says they have hung themselves, and were found hanging, clasping each other's hands. Their father who is a colonel in the army left his wife many years ago. What misery they must have experienced, poor things!

I suppose you want to know how I am, don't you? Well, I cannot say I am *well* but better. The doctor was here today and says I am doing very well so I shall be very well next week. I am neither "thin, pale, or delicate looking." So you see, love, or you might if you were here, that I have not been very ill, only not well. Mother is also better, but a little. Mr. Hains gives us no hope of her recovery. He says it is not in the power of any medicine to make her well but if he can make her better, it will be a great thing.

Alicia is looking forward to the end of this year with happy thoughts and gleeful anticipations when in all possibility Spencer will arrive. What a meeting that will be!

He has been away nearly ten years! What a change they will each see in the other!

How happy am I that I can see you at least once a year; would that it could be oftener! But patience and confidence and hope stand me in the stead of your loved presence.

Good night, dearest,
Yours only,
Addey

Everybody's love

Grim futures awaited many of the women who had no means of supporting themselves. The three Watson sisters marry well in a time when marriage was the primary means to economic security. All outlived their husbands.

18 March 1851 64 Bartholomew Close

My dearest Addey,

Thank you for your last. It was a regular long one & no mistake & more resembling those you used to send me. You are a most excellent dear little soul, you know. I am quite delighted to know your illness has not made you pale & thin for I imagined it would have done so. You will soon be quite well, dear, but mind you don't go out too soon & take fresh cold.

Do you notice I am writing all cramped like? I went over to little Dr. Hodgkins to breakfast this morning & while the maid was getting it ready, of course, we must be up to some mischief & I must needs shew Hodgy a new pass in fencing which I thought I knew. George Little makes the thrust with a cane & the Doctor in parrying (with a *breakfast knife*) managed to give my sword hand a nice chop right across the back of my little finger. 'Tis a nasty, deep sort of cut, but fortunately it did not cut the sinew of my finger or I probably should have lost the use of my hand altogether. As it is, I can only write with much difficulty. I've got a bit of lint & sticking plaster on so it will be all right in a day or two. Only you know 'tis just another proof of what a great, awkward, careless youth I am & how you can make up your mind to be contented with such a goose as I am, often makes me wonder much. You are too good for me, Addey. You are a little darling & I couldn't think of you loving anyone but me for the world. Selfish, you see.

And this pretty little friend of yours; is she really as interesting as you say? If so, & she is with you when I come down, I know you will have some trouble with me. I'm not proof against little ladies with laughing eyes. I can't stand 'em at all. You know how you have tied me up yourself with those wicked, blue eyes of your own. I should like to see them now very much.

Poor Carter! Alas, alas, he's *finished this morning* yes, *married* – unfortunate man. I am invited down to Clampitts this evening – to condole with the bereaved uncle & aunt & drink success to the newly married couple – over a bottle of wine. This part of the ceremony I intend to perform with much gusto & determination. I wonder when we shall be married, Addey, I wish 'twas now, I do!

Oh, my hand – such a twinge. I must leave off, dear. Good bye, kiss me,

Ever thine unalterably,
Geo L. Virtue

I won't fence anymore then, I'm always being hurt or getting the worst of it somehow.

George describes himself as "a great, awkward, careless youth" in his humorous account of his high jinks with friend Hodgie and resulting wound. His flair for the written word suggests he might have been better suited to the literary side of publishing.

His reaction to Addey's "lady with the laughing eyes" reveals his ever flirtatious eye.

13 May 1851 64 Bartholomew Close

My dear little Addey,

You are a good little soul, as ever, but you mustn't keep me without my letter of a Sunday for it makes me quite unhappy. Now, what a selfish unfeeling bear I am, don't you think so? Of course, I know you had the wish to send me the letter in time only something turned up to prevent its being posted – or so I reason to conclude.

Yet if you will (when practicable) post it on Friday afternoons, 'twould be setting a fellow's mind at rest all Sunday. I would kiss you into order if I were at Bowdon but as I am not – why then – when I don't hear from you as I expect, 'tis like just a faint glimpse of the anguish I should feel at losing my little Addey altogether.

Larry Drew is come home – as big as a house and strong as a lion – which I can testify to by sundry bruises on my arm from having a turn at single stick with him down at Jem's one evening. I went with him to see his brother Codner on Sunday, who is in a little business for himself about ten miles from here in a very nice little village called Merton, in Surrey. We spent a pleasant day talking over old times – and by way of a finish I had to walk home (or run for I only had an hour & a half) the next morning which gave me an appetite for breakfast surely. I expect he will be going down to Devonshire about the same time I intend leaving, so we shall be company going down. After then no more company shall I desire than my good darling Addey, bless her heart.

Your reasons for not wishing to leave with me were quite good & proper & I am only prouder of you for expressing them. I like to hear you say you love me – like making honey sweeter.

Well, now, my son, let me go, there's a dear. You know how much we have to talk about when I come down – & shall I ask the Governor if we shall be married next year, eh? I should walk to church on my hands for joy, I'm sure.

Good bye, love. Now try to write a letter before Monday,

Ever your own,
George

What a captivating image – you walking to the church on your hands for joy – if "the Governor" would agree to your marrying Addey in the next year. Your warmth, humor, and kind and loving nature are irresistible, George, though I probably would not have kept you in line as Addey did and as you wished her to.

What a strange and random business, this determining of who we select for our life partners. I am grateful beyond measure that you and Addey found one another, which in turn assured my existence 170 years later and the chance to eavesdrop on the intimacy of your courtship.

28 May 1851 64 Bartholomew Close

My dear little Addey,

How sorry I am for your disappointment this morning at not receiving this letter, but when I tell you I could not possibly spare time to write before, I'm sure your gentle spirit will pardon & forgive me, won't you now like a good girl as you are.

I have no one to assist me here this week so you see I am well pressed for time, magazine week & all.

Thank you for the seeds. I have no doubt they will produce very pretty flowers, but such is my ignorance of botany that I haven't the slightest conception of what kind they are. However I must have patience & wait till they come up & then I suppose I shall know more about 'em.

I commenced doing up my garden last week. Jem Glanville got up early to come & help me, but the ground was so fearfully hard (Jem said he got into a strata of brickbats) that we did not make much progress, but I shall turn out tomorrow morning & put it in some shape for it is awfully out of order at present.

Addey's father and brother supported their families by having plant nurseries. A fondness and talent for growing plants has continued to the present day. My grandparents had a large garden of flowers and vegetables, tended, I might add, by a paid gardener. My mother was a consummate gardener.

It is hard to imagine a garden anywhere in the vicinity of Bartholomew Close today, as modern office buildings densely line the traffic-filled streets. The Close itself is a short semi-circular street, now taken up by a hospital. At the far end was a small church which was fenced off because it was undergoing restoration. Not far from the Close, with old and new maps in hand, I found another of the old addresses, Paternoster Row, which was formerly the publishing heart of London. It is now only Roman capitals carved into a concrete slab at a busy intersection. I did find Ivy Lane behind St. Paul's, where Virtue & Company had stood originally. This section was bombed out during the Second World War, and much archival material was destroyed.

Oh, I think I shall be able to come down sooner than I expected. I hope to leave London either on Thursday or Friday week. I am not sure whether I shall not have to go to Plymouth on business, in which case I shall go down by water all the way. Larry Drew will come down with me he says, but as his ship will sail on the 20th of next month, he will have to leave before me. Another fortnight & I shall be with my little darling again. Hurrah. Good bye, dear,

In a dreadful hurry (as usual)
Ever yours,
Geo L Virtue

Kind love to all

5 June 1851 — 64 Bartholomew Close

My dearest Addey,

I have delayed writing to you before on purpose that I might tell you when for certain I should leave.

I start tomorrow morning by the steamer for Plymouth & I hope to reach Bowdon either on Sunday evening or the first thing on Monday morning. I must return to London the latter end of next week – it has cost me some time & trouble to get leave even for so short a stay. Never mind, only two days more & I shall be with my own darling little Addey, hurrah. When you get this tomorrow morning Larry & I will be rolling about in the Channel – fair weather & a speedy trip, pray I.

Good bye, dearest,
Ever your own,
George

George "rolling about" made it to Devon, staying there from June 7th to June 14th. They never mention what they did, though of course there was no need, as both were there. They weren't aware that one of their descendants so many years hence would be curious. I'm sure there were moonlight strolls and daytime walks, as well as visits with friends and Addey's family and precious time alone together. The week must have gone by much too quickly.

9 July 1851 Bowdon

My dearest George,

You will be surprised to receive a letter from me before the appointed time, but the truth is, love, I am going to Plymouth tomorrow by the first train and if I do not write tonight the chance is against your getting a letter this week, which I know would not please my dear, particular George. I cannot tell you how long I shall be away, not more than two or three weeks, I suppose. I don't care one bit about going at all. And truth to say, I would quite as soon remain at home. I do not like visiting as much as I used to. I am steadier, I think – no longer "fancy free" as you know. Therein is the difference, I imagine.

So you think I was suspicious when I made enquiry about the stock-taking? I assure you, you are mistaken in that thought for I know it to be a necessary piece of business, and simply and innocently asked the question. Alas, alas! That we should be so misunderstood. But indeed, dearest, I do not mistrust you. You *know* I do not and if you are wayward sometimes, you *know* you are all the world to your little Addey.

You gave me a sort of hint about the shortness of my last letter and I very much fear this will be no longer. I have been busy packing, and it is not now quite finished, but I will say, as you have said, I will write again this week if I have time.

Thank you, my hand is quite well. I will promise to be more careful in the future for my own sake, for I don't like pain at all. It was a bit of carelessness, 'tis sure. Would I blow you up if it had been you? Well, perhaps I might, but "you couldn't be cross" with me if you "wanted to be." Well! I have no wish for you to be, for it makes me very wretched.

I hope to write a longer letter next week. This though is longer than yours, so you can't find fault.

Mother, I am quite happy to say, is better. All else are well. So are you, I hope. Good night, dearest,

Dream of your own,
Ever true,
Addey

Addey does gad about, but she realizes full well George gets upset when he doesn't hear from her on schedule.

11 August 1851 — 64 Bartholomew Close

My dear Addey,

Fancy I have been asleep or dead or something of that kind for the last week. I will not pretend to offer any excuse for my silence, so do be merciful, do.

During the last fortnight I really have had more to do & more country friends calling to see me than all the rest of the exhibition time put together, & I must tell you, there have been a number of ladies among them, old, young, pretty & so so. Therefore, my dear Addey, I will leave you to imagine how much I have been engaged lately.

I hope you have had better weather. It must be very tiresome to have had such a deal of wet weather, but rain in Cornwall is proverbial, my dear, so you must not let it make you cross.

I spent an evening at Carter Godfrey's last week. He has a nice little house about a mile & a half from the city. I met Sarah Taylor there & I made her a sort of half promise I would call & take her out for a walk to see Exeter Hall.

In the midst of all my hustle and excitement, I managed to have a rather severe touch of influenza. However, I am all right again & if little Addey won't be *too cross,* I'll promise to be a better boy in future & more punctual in answering letters.

Yours,
Geo. L. Virtue

Crystal Palace, 1851

The Crystal Palace Exhibition

The visitors George is undoubtedly referring to when he mentions "a number of ladies, among them old, young, pretty, & so so," are those who came to London to see the Crystal Palace Exhibition, which opened on May 1st, 1851. Its formal name was The Great Exhibition of the Works of All Industry of All Nations, a name outdone only by the extent of its myriad displays. Housed in an immense glass greenhouse designed by Joseph Paxton, a former gardener for the Earl of Devonshire, it enclosed sixteen acres containing fully grown trees and enormous fountains, plus exhibits of the emerging technology and engineering achievements of the day. In addition were replicas of the Alhambra, the Temple of Karnak, an Assyrian palace, and a Pompeiian house. Freak shows, circus acts, stuffed wild animals, the Koh i Noor diamond – with its accompanying curse – were all on view. Copies of nude male Roman statues caused a mild stir and a last-minute search for plaster fig leaves. The Exhibition had the first public toilets.

Albert, Prince Consort, was actively involved with the conception and implementation of the event. Other nations were invited to participate, though the primary goal was to highlight Britain's preeminence and impress the world with her scientific achievements. By all accounts it proved successful beyond the highest expectations. The new network of railroads brought visitors from all over England at the rate of 42,000 a day.

Queen Victoria, too, was a frequent visitor. She came early before the crowds and was as captivated as her subjects.

Friday morning

My dearest George,

I have been practicing for so long that I am frightened to see the time. But I am happy to give you a better account of Mother. Since Monday she has been getting better and we are beginning to cherish a hope of her recovery. It will indeed be wonderful if she does. Father also, who has been very ill, is improved and will in a few days be well.

I received a very kind letter from Annie on Tuesday which I hope to answer in a day or two. I am very glad your brother is getting better. I should like to know him and I suppose I shall some day. Meantime give my love to him.

I cannot say anything about the time of my visiting London until I know when Compton will be home. Most probably it will be sometime *this* year. How long I shall stay I cannot tell. Perhaps a month. It is not likely that I shall be able to be away from home for a longer period than that. Oh, how about the portrait, Mr. George? I wonder when I am to have it. I think I have been remarkably patient about it, don't you? Well then, I deserve to be rewarded, don't I? When shall I be, eh? If I were near you, I would coax you into saying, "It shall be soon."

Sarah Taylor is in raptures with the Exhibition and all the sights she saw in London and would "so like to live there." She likes the place, the noise, the bustle, and above all, she likes the Londoners! Then, she did not meet very many and those with which she was made acquainted were very pleasant people. Truly she must have enjoyed herself marvelously. She was sorry to come home again.

Well now, my own love, I must say goodbye for this must be concluded. Oh! George, you don't know how much I love you! That was quite involuntary, so you must prize it all the more.

Goodbye,
Ever your own,
Addey

16 SEPTEMBER 1851 64 BARTHOLOMEW CLOSE

My dearest Addey,

I am delighted to hear Mother is better & I sincerely trust she will keep on mending until she has so far recovered as to put you past all apprehensions for her.

What delightful weather it has been this month. It makes one feel good all through. I wish my leave of absence was still to come. How much I should like to be coming down to Totnes, say tomorrow, & to take our old customary walks by moonlight. Ah me, I often think of those happy times, Addey. I wonder if we shall ever spend many more such but of course, we shall. Only I was thinking that London is not exactly the place to enjoy quiet rambles like we used to have & I am afraid (if you will have me in spite of all my faults) you must make up your mind to like living in London, or rather to endure doing so, for I cannot believe anyone with natural taste would prefer living in London to the country for long. Sarah Taylor says she could always wish to live here. Yes, but she would soon grow tired after the novelty & excitement had worn away the charm, however. After all, London is the place to get on. (I feel sure of that & also, that I can do better here than anywhere else.)

Oh, do you know I am turned religious again. I went to church Sunday & intend to continue doing so every week. I always feel better after a good sermon & therefore I must take that as proof that I am benefited thereby – selfish, you see, even in this.

My likeness, what a long-promised gift, to be sure. I'm quite ashamed of myself when I think how patient you have been, but it was not altogether my fault either. The artist who promised to do it for me has been on a tour, & since his return his wife has died & I do not like to bother him just now. Would a daguerreotype please you for the present? Your image is graven deep on my heart but still I should like to have a little likeness of you very much. I regret we did not think about it when we were in Torquay the other day. We could have had 'em both taken then. Stop till you come to London. You will consent to sit for one then, won't you, love?

Jem Glanville has just called in inviting me to go with him & the Messrs. Clampitt & Manley to a discussion this evening, so if I mean to go I must look sharp & get through my day's work to be on time.

So my dear little Addey, you must pardon my giving in.

Ever your own,
GLV

P.S. Brother Tom is coming up tomorrow to see the Exhibition & Ted (who is better) sends his love to Addey. I suppose so much illness at home has prevented the Governor from looking out for a partridge or so this season. How I should like to come down for a week to see Addey and – shoot partridges.

Love to all.

FRIDAY BOWDON

[Addey to George]

I am afraid my dearest George that I shall have no means of sending this in to the post even if I write to you, for I suppose you know by this time that I am here alone with the invalids and cannot leave them. The consequence is you will be disappointed, I fear.

Yes, Alicia is positively gone to London after all. I was afraid when she left that they would have wet weather for their visit but it has proved to be a needless fear for 'tis beautiful, only rather cold. Winter is coming on rapidly. Dear me! What a long time it is since you were here. I wish I could see you oftener, but it is of no use wishing. I suppose whatever is, is right as the old doctor said yesterday. He says Father is better. He hopes to "get him sound again now." Mother is also a little better, and I trust now they will both recover.

And am I to have the likeness soon, *really* not only a promise but the veritable portrait? I suppose, dear, you will give it to Alicia? To bring home to me, I mean. You know, she will be here again next Thursday. How much I should have liked to have gone with her, but it could not be. And I am afraid I shall not go this year after all. Compton is "afraid" he shall not be able to be home this year, not until early in the next. Stupid fellow, isn't he? (What a terrible business business is! Pity people can't do without it, eh?) But you must not think I shall be sorry when he does come, for I shall *not*. She will be very glad, of course, and so also shall I, however sorry I may be to lose her. We shall not look upon her like again. Were you not surprised to see her, for I suppose you have seen her before this. She said she could call today. I wish I were with her! I am being constantly called away to attend to the wants of the invalids. I cannot sit still five minutes at a time, so if there are many blunders it is not to be wondered at.

We had a letter from Winnie this week. She and all of them are very well and she desires her love to you.

You said in your last, dearest, that you are pale and thin and that you had a "little bit of a cold." Now, you know, a little bit of a cold would not have such a distressing effect on you. Just you tell me exactly what it is that is making you "pale and thin." I know you don't take care enough of yourself. I wish I were there to make you. I am always so frightened at the thought of your being ill *there* where you have nobody to nurse and watch over you. Are you very pale and thin? But I shall know from Alicia. I daresay you will tell me it is nothing or nonsense. Well then, my own love, don't get ill until I am with you to nurse you. Now you needn't laugh for I can assure you I am a capital nurse. I *know* nobody would tend *you* so well.

Now I hope you are not very much disappointed this morning, for you must know I put this away yesterday. I could not send it till it was too late. And now you have a long letter, very closely written. Are you not very grateful to me for writing so much when yours was so short?

Goodbye now, dear,
Your own,
Addey

SUNDAY BOWDON

My dearest George,

I am once more writing you from Bowdon. We arrived about six o'clock. I was very tired and so glad to see Totnes Station. That is, you know, I was not tired of being in London, only wearied with the journey. And this morning I was so glad to get the portrait. It seems to be even more like you now than it was in London. You were very good to send it on so soon. They all say it is an admirable likeness.

I was very glad to find Father much better than when I left, but poor Mother is not nearly so well.

I wonder where you are now. You were engaged to have breakfast with Hodgkins, I think. I suppose you are with him somewhere – a dreadful fancy man you are, I am afraid.

By the way, do you know what they did with my carpet bag? Because I don't. It was not with the rest of the luggage yesterday, but Mr. Bastin is going to make enquiries about it for me. How was it directed? I shall send out by and by when I hope to obtain some intelligence concerning it.

I cannot write very much for I am feeling very unsettled, but the next shall be longer so I hope yours will be also. I have so much to think about – the events of the last week. I have not yet told Father of your going to America. Just hinted at it last night, but found I had better say no more for the time being.

Good bye, will you write soon, that I may hear on Wednesday?

Your ever,
Addey

Everybody's love

And suddenly life changes dramatically for the young couple. Addey has learned that George is to be sent to the U.S. by Virtue & Company, this time, it seems, for certain. How lightly George speaks of going off to seek his fortune, something he has sought since he went to London.

And I cannot help but muse on how our fates are determined by when we arrive on this curious stage we call life, and to whom we are attracted, and with whom we choose to share our lives.

It is strange to contemplate, and stranger still to acknowledge how vivid the two of you are to me. You certainly are present in my mind's eye, which causes me to wonder about this short time each of us spends here on earth. Somehow, my knowledge of you helps me to confront my own mortality as I approach a time when I will depart this world.

I love her calling George "a dreadful fancy man." They delight in teasing each other.

SUNDAY MORNING BOWDON

My own dearest George,

Many thanks for your nice long letter. We have just received our foreign news and I am very much disappointed at some of the intelligence from Compton. You know we all thought and he gave Alicia to understand that he was coming home soon to reside. Now it appears his visit will be but for a time, in fact only to fetch her! And he hopes to be home before Christmas, although he thinks it doubtful as he cannot get anybody to take care of his affairs during his absence. Isn't it dreadful? Poor Alicia was quite taken aback. This will be a great deal worse than Winnie's going to India. A most unhappy arrangement. I wonder if she will go? I suppose of course she will. It was sad enough to think of her going away, when we thought she would live in London! And I had almost gained Father's consent to my going to America. Alas, alas! It is very strange that all three of us should leave England, is it not?

> *As Addey comments on her sister Alicia's prolonged engagement and subsequent marriage, she may be thinking with some trepidation about the possibility of her joining George, when she will leave her parents, her friends, and the beautiful Devon countryside which both she and George love so much.*

I think, my dear George, you are as good a fellow as I think you, although you seem to doubt it. I know you are a darling. No! I am *sure* there's *nobody* like my own, dearest George. What would I do without you, but then you are going away! Well, never mind, dearest, you won't forget your Addey, and it won't be forever, as you say. I am beginning to fear you will have a disagreeable voyage for winter is coming. I hope it won't be stormy, but I mustn't meet trouble halfway as you used to tell me.

Give my love to Ted. I am glad he is so much better. I too was disappointed at not seeing Mrs. Lawrence. However, I hope I shall some day. I wish you were not going until Compton comes home for I shall not like to be in London and you not there – if I go – I may not.

Mother sends her love to you. She says she hopes she shall see you. She is frightfully weak, yet I think, on the whole, a little better. Who knows?

Your picture is such a treasure, not that it makes me think of you at all more frequently. Neither does it help me to recall your features and expression for I can think of the latter even better when I am not looking at it. Yet it is much to have those we love brought as it were tangibly before us, and I do love you oh so much.

Goodbye, my George. This is not a very long letter, I know, but you will pardon your own little

Addey

And believe I am always thinking of you.

Virtue & Company

George might be gratified to know that Virtue & Company continued until recently, when Michael Virtue, the last family member to head it, sold the name and lists to the Yorkshire firm E. Russum & Sons, Ltd. Michael had taken the firm over from his father, Guy, who in turn had taken it over from his father, Herbert. It had remained in the hands of the Virtue family since it was established in 1813 by the original George Virtue, for whom our George worked.

On my first visit to Europe in 1952, I often visited Virtue & Company Ltd., a name which evoked smiles from those who wrote to me there. Guy Virtue was then head of the firm, and took me under his wing. It was a home away from home, where I picked up mail and was given help navigating the exigencies of living abroad. The office was then in Holborn. It was lined with high shelves of books, many of them the volumes of the lives of the saints they were publishing at the time. They had managed to keep afloat during the difficult post-war period by putting out an authorized Catholic Bible, which sold profitably there and here. Later on they did well with books for professional chefs. I have a copy of *Ancient Stone Crosses of England*, illustrated with seventy-two fine engravings.

Many of these crosses were constructed in the Middle Ages, some before, and fulfilled a variety of purposes, religious and secular.

Mary Ottoway, Guy's capable assistant, took a motherly interest in my European adventures. She gently suggested to me one Friday afternoon that it was not a prudent plan to rent a bicycle in Battersea to ride to Cornwall. I, who was raised on the misleading notion of England's small size – at least in comparison to the U.S. – thought the trip would take a mere two or three days. My first comeuppance was being shunted with the rented bike to the baggage car in the back of the train I had boarded to get out of the city. It was only the kindness of a proper British gentleman, who introduced himself on the train as Flight Commander Price, which resulted in my finding a bed for a night in Andover, where I arrived to complete darkness at 9 p.m. He directed me to a B&B not far from the railroad station owned by a friend of his. With assists from other forms of transportation – trains and boats and a few bicycle rides – I arrived at St. Mawes a week later, enlightened as to the distances involved and other challenges of English life.

31 October 1851 Bowdon

My beloved George,

What glorious weather. How much I wish you were here to enjoy it. I can hardly fancy winter is so near at hand. This has been a wonderfully short summer and autumn. I think it seems to be so from the fact of my having been away from home so much, I suppose. Ah well! I must settle down quietly some time, eh? When I am a few years older.

Is your heart at rest about going away yet, dearest? I hope you know for certain one way or the other, and if you are going, for nothing is so tantalizing and disagreeable as suspense. I hope after all you will go because, dearest, I believe if it is decided otherwise, you will be disappointed. *Therefore*, I hope you will go. *However* it is to be, we must hope it will be well, as you say and I believe you. You are a dear boy, but you know that already, don't you?

Alicia is going to take this in for me. She intended going yesterday, but you see I was very unwell indeed, so she could not. And truth to tell, I am not very well today. 'Tis only a pretty severe cold so I shall be all right tomorrow.

A month ago, what were my – our – feelings? Very different from what they are now. I was expecting to see you on the morrow. What changes we sometimes see in only one little month. Now I am almost constantly thinking and sometimes saying to myself, "He is going away." Now you need not laugh. The thought is constantly before me, and I confess it sometimes makes me feel very sad and lonely. But I daresay that is not right so I won't say any more about it, for I know wherever you are, you are my own dear George, and you won't love me less for having the waters of the Atlantic between us, will you dearest? And your little Addey will always be true and faithful, you know.

I am sorry I cannot say Mother improves. She is not so well. She sends her love, and so do the rest. Alicia is waiting.

Ever your own,
Addey

➣ *Addey reveals what is in her heart as she faces a separation far longer in time and greater in distance than those she and George have already gone through. The possibility of this being a final separation must have crossed her mind. Even though she writes that George won't love her any less for having the waters of the Atlantic between them, it must have occurred to her that its watery depths could easily swallow him up.*

But what if you had not come to these shores, George? How might your life (and mine) have been affected if you had stayed in London? All those descendants between you and me on either side of the Atlantic prompt me to ask what a different fate might have resulted.

Memories are leaky vessels. So much vanishes without a trace, but through the survival of these letters, these seemingly fragile words, preserved on tissue-thin paper, have outlasted the flesh and blood individuals who created them, and have achieved an immortality of their own.

11 November 1851 — 64 Bartholomew Close

My dearest Addey,

I have only time to send an apology for a note this time.

Mr. John Bain (my successor) has arrived today. He is a canny Scotchman. How long before I can make him understand things here, I don't know. I had hoped to be finished this week, but I am afraid it will not be quite so soon.

I have said nothing to Uncle about wishing to go home to say goodbye to all. I still hope to be able to do so.

I intended going from Southampton by the *Rembrandt*, an American steamer. She will sail *Thursday week*, but I shall know more about it in another day or two.

I will write again as soon as I can. Let me hear from you by Saturday, there's a darling.

Goodbye
Love ever yours,
Geo L. Virtue

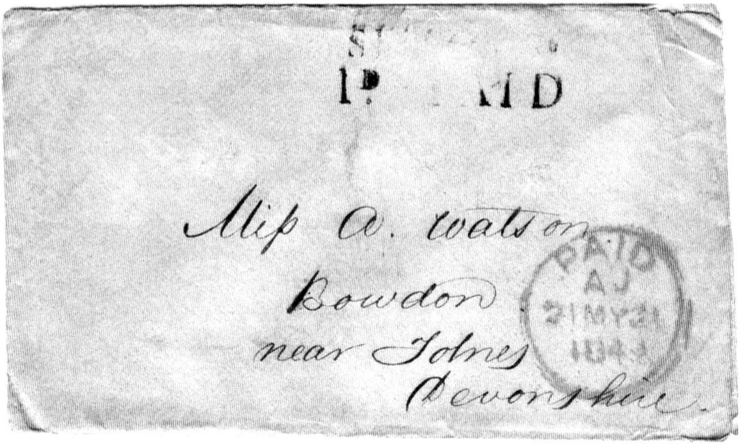
PAID
AJ
Miss A. Watson
Bowdon
near Totnes
Devonshire

18
Mr George L. Virtue
64 Bartholomew Close
Smithfield
London

PART III

George in America

U.S. postage stamp, issued 2011.

Text on the reverse side of the stamp reads: "Auxiliary steamships—steam-powered ships with back-up sailing rigs—were the ocean liners of their day, competing in the 1850s with clipper and other sailing ships for transatlantic mail and passenger service."

1852

The world is a book which I have only commenced learning to read

Addey's fear that George would have a stormy voyage proved well-founded. On December 5th George sailed from Liverpool on the *City of Pittsburgh*, one of the new hybrid steamships, still equipped with sailing apparatus, fortunately. A screw propeller broke soon after their departure, and they were forced to continue under sail. George describes the perilous seven-week voyage in his first letter of 1852. I hope Addey was able to read the journal he kept of the trip. It was not with the letters.

13 January 1852

On board steamship
City of Pittsburgh
Delaware Bay

My dearest Addey,

I shall write these few lines to you, my dear, with more pleasure than I have ever written to you before. It does seem so long since I heard from you. I can only say I am alive & well for the boat will leave to take the letters almost directly. We have had a very bad passage indeed. Three days after we left Liverpool, we lost our screw propeller so we were compelled to make the rest of the voyage under canvas. The Captain would have gone back, but in consequence of the accident, the ship would not answer her helm. The Captain was afraid we should be run onto a lee shore so he determined to keep out at sea.

I have kept up my journal as well as I could & will send it to you in my next letter which I shall write as soon as I get on shore. We are detained here until the weather breaks up the ice. The river is frozen in & here we are lying at anchor for an indefinite period. Well, I don't care much about it now for we are near enough to a small town (Lewistown) to get provisions and other necessaries so we do not have much to complain of except the severe cold which is most intense. My fingers are like icicles. Just now I wish I could get a sight of you. It would warm me all over. When I come over to fetch you, my dear Addey, I'll take care it shall be in the summer. There is a newly married couple on board: an American gentleman who came to England & is now returning with an English wife (she, poor thing, seems truly downhearted & miserable & considering we have been on board seven weeks tomorrow in the very worst kind of weather, she has every reason to be unhappy).

Goodbye then, dear Addey, for the present. Write to me as soon as you receive this & tell me all the news. I am almost afraid to ask how poor Mother is, but I hope & trust you will be enabled to tell me she is better. Give my kind love to her & Father & Alicia & all inquiring friends & believe me to be, dear Addey,

Ever yours sincerely,
George L. Virtue

Write to me at Messrs Virtue & Company
26 John Street
New York
Send me out a paper – if you can get one (*Bell's Life*!).

Blown off course with an unplanned leg to South America, it must have been a terrifying voyage. Finally reaching the shores of the new world made even the freezing over of the ship in the ice of Delaware Bay seem inconsequential. What a harsh introduction to George's new life in this country!

30 JANUARY 1852 BOWDON

My dearest George,

I can hardly convey to you an idea of the delight with which I received this so long expected letter. It is but just brought. I have been fancying all sorts of terrible things to account for its long delay. At last it is come and I find that my darling George has been exposed to dangers and storms although you do not say so, but I know it must have been so. We have had rather stormy weather here, but not so bad as you have had at sea. But you are safe and I am happy. I am so glad, dearest, that you have kept a diary, so kind it is of you.

Where should I ever find one *half so good* and kind as you are? Do I not love you more than all the world? I cannot tell you how I have longed to see you since you have been away for, dearest, I have been in sorrow. You will be grieved, I know, although not much surprised to know that I have no longer a mother. You know that it is a hard thing to lose a mother, one that has been ever kind and whom we have ever and always loved. She died on the very morning your last letter (dated from Liverpool) arrived on the 9th of December. She very much regretted not seeing you again, and a day or two before she died, she called me to her and said, "Addey, when you write to him, give my love, my best love to George, dear boy. I am sorry I did not see him before he left but he will always be kind to you without my injunction, 'tis his nature. God bless him, God bless you both. Be a true wife, my child, and may you be happy together!" She bade me, dearest, tell you what she said. She was so happy, and so patient under all her sufferings, so uncomplaining and she so longed for death. She is blessed and we cannot for a moment wish her back with us, remembering what she suffered, for although happily the pain was not great, yet for her it was a long weary illness, and truly her end was peace.

The death of your mother, Addey, was no less hard for being expected. You must have taken some consolation in the closeness of your family and felt in a small degree heartened by the care you gave her during her last days, as well as the comfort of being with her at the end. Years later, these were the words Winnie used to describe her: "Strictly just, always true to her word; tender, loving, and calm. She looked on the bright side and never scolded. Encouraged her children to attend to the poor." The loss of one's

> *mother is always profound. Long after you too had left this earth, I learned from my grandfather, your son Herbert, that you had many of your mother's exemplary maternal qualities. Herbert always spoke of you with great affection, referring to you as "little mother."*

I was surprised to find from your letter that the cold was so severe. Why we have had no frost whatever, hardly a hoar frost. And now it is quite mild enough to sit with the windows open. I wonder if you have been released from your frozen captivity yet? Poor lady, I mean the bride. I dare say she thought it very dreadful, such a cold reception. I think I should prefer arriving there in the summer, but I would keep up my spirits, even amidst frost and snow. And you don't tell me if you have been ill or not. Were you? I should have liked to have been able to have looked in on you once – no, not once, but as often as I liked. It must be a very nice thing to be clairvoyant, I fancy. If I were, I wonder what I should see you doing now? But what is the use of allowing one's imagination to run wild? It *is* pleasant though, sometimes. I have been wanting so much to write to you, but if I could not write, I did not forget, and, dearest, if I had not had you to think of, I should have been very unhappy. It is so sweet to feel there is one who loves me. And whom I love, oh how dearly, but I am talking of myself again.

You want to know all the news. Verily, I don't think there is any. Alicia is still with us. Compton will be home either in April or June. Father still continues very unwell indeed. Yet I think he is getting better since he has changed his doctor. He is hunting now. He talks of going to Barnet for a change of air. He will be very glad when he knows you have written. He has amused himself by teazing me, telling me you had forgotten me, and I should never hear from you again and all that sort of thing, which of course passed unheeded, for I knew it was not so.

Alicia thinks I am writing quite a "foreign letter," and alas, you are in a foreign land. Well, I suppose such is life, all change. Winnie is very well, and sends her best love to you. Always we receive sunny letters from her telling of love and happiness. They are indeed happy, and so shall we be, shall we not, dearest? Alicia says she is almost as glad that I have had a letter as I am myself – though not quite, I think. And when the next comes, I shall be so glad. I hope you will like it there. Tell me all about it. Everything you can think of. You know, love, everything connected with you is of the greatest interest to me, and ever must be.

Good bye, my beloved George. I am always thinking of you and am ever your own true

Addey

Sunday evening

You see, dearest, I took this to the post on Friday, As it happened, most unfortunately, the packet left on that very day. So of course I was one day too late, and consequently am obliged to wait another week. And you will have a somewhat longer letter, although I think it is not now very short. I wonder where you are now. I should so like to know, but as I cannot, I am reduced to fancy.

I think, my love, I am rather prosy tonight and as I have several letters which I must, or ought, to write, I will put this away for the time. I fear you will be tired of this long before you have waded through it. I only wish you would send me such long letters, but you will write longer ones now than of yore, I know. Hmm! Goodnight, dear.

Wednesday

This then is the last day and I must finish the letter and again take it to the office.

And so, dearest, you have been to *South* America! Very much surprised was I at the intelligence. You must have had a much worse passage than you told me. If I had known how you were tossed about, and in what danger you were, I wonder if I should have felt very comfortable. But you are now safe, and have been a far greater traveller than you anticipated – or wished. I suppose you are curious to know how I became informed of your having been to Buenos Aires. You will, I imagine, open your eyes when I tell you, from your uncle! No, I did not write to be informed, but I know from the said gentleman that they have not heard from you, but have obtained intelligence of the steamer and in part knew more than I who have heard from you. And now, dearest, let me thank you for writing to me so soon. You are indeed good and I know I cannot love you too much. And Jem, partly I suppose to satisfy his curiosity, and partly to relieve my anxiety, called at the Close, where he obtained the information from Mrs. Virtue. So you see, although I knew from your uncle, it was indirectly.

Now then, my love, once more, farewell. Alicia's love and all of your own

Addey

And how relieved and happy you must have been to get his letter telling of his safe arrival.

9 February 1852 26 John Street, New York

[George to Addey]

After all my troubles I once more have the pleasing duty of writing to my dearest Addey. I landed first at Philadelphia where I remained until last Friday week when I came on to New York and have been here ever since. I shall likely remain here for two or three months, or at all events, until the winter has broken up, when I expect to make my first trip to Cincinnati. I cannot give you much information about America yet for I have seen but little of the country, but what I have seen, I have been much pleased with, and entertain a different idea of the place altogether to what I have been led to imagine from reading Mrs. Trollope's work, or Dickens' *Martin Chuzzlewit.*

New York is a splendid city crowded with magnificent hotels and public buildings, most of them built of marble, which gives them a most noble appearance. The main street, Broadway, is nearly three miles long and full of fine shops, or stores as they call them here. The people are a motley race indeed, from the fact of so many emigrants constantly flocking over, but the regular inhabitants are a very orderly and respectable looking crowd and far more gentlemanly and pleasing in their manners than I expected to find them. The ladies, most of them, are what folks would call good-looking, or even beautiful, yet they do not please my fancy. They are too sallow and attenuated to please me but I have not had much opportunity to judge of their manners. My cousin James says he will introduce me to some charming little creatures if I would like to go with him, but I am in no humour to be charmed by them. Just now I have come over here to work hard and save money and it shall go hard with me if I do not succeed. I have taken pleasant "board" in Brooklyn, Long Island, which gives me a walk of about two miles out every morning and two miles home at night. The only luxury I allow myself is a cigar. You must not wish to debar me of that, will you?

I was laid up for a few days in Philadelphia and after so much pitching and tossing about I am sure it was enough to make anyone queer. I will not say too much against the sea though or I shall hardly tempt you to venture over with me when I return to England to fetch you, which I mean to do if you will wait for me so long. I wonder when I shall be going up Bowdon Hill again with my heart as light as a feather. Dear old Bowdon, there is no spot in the world I like to think of so much as it – and then the dearest, best of girls. But I won't say any more or else you will say I'm growing sentimental like Mr. Toots.

Well, do you know, Addey, I have not received a single letter or paper from any of my friends in England. I almost expected one from you but seeing you didn't know where to write, it was hardly likely. However, you must write me no end of a letter directly you receive this. Mind, tell me all the news. I hope your poor mother is better. My kind love to them all.

I saw Lola Montez in Philadelphia. She is a beautiful woman certainly, but thin and a bad danseuse.

I wrote to you while we were lying off Cape Penelope at the mouth of the Delaware. Did you receive it? On the other side, I send you a copy of my journal which you made me promise to keep, but the composition and altogether it seems such an absurd, frivolous thing that I shall be ashamed for you to read it to anyone. I am not clever at journal keeping, so pray don't ask me to write one again unless you are better pleased with this specimen than I am myself.

So good bye, Addey dear. Keep your heart up and continue to love and remember

Yours ever affectionately,
George L Virtue

Having been in the U.S. for less than a month, George is pleased with much of what he sees, though he is still missing England, Bowdon, and, of course, most of all, his beloved Addey, whom he teases with his cousin James' taunts. Mid-nineteenth-century America is as unknown to me as it was to you, George, when you arrived. I am captivated by your descriptions of the city and its inhabitants.

There is a gap of three months before the next letter from Addey. The frequency of the letters has diminished with the increased distance between them. Although there are fewer letters, they are longer and more intense.

12 May 1852 Bowdon

My dearest George,

I have waited till the very last day expecting and hoping for a letter from you. Why is this long silence? It is now nearly two months since I had the happiness of receiving a letter from my own George. It is a weary time to wait. I have been patient, but lately I have grown fearful, of what? Not of your truth, dearest, no, not for an instant, but of your safety and health. I have seen in the papers accounts of such dreadful accidents. Steamers having blown up, such terrific storms by which oh! so many have been killed, and all happening near New York. One steamer blew up on her way from that place to Cincinnati, and you told me you were going there. Is it not possible that you were one of her passengers? And, oh God! may it not be that at this moment, you are *not*, that you are lost to me forever. What then is left for me but to die too. But I pray heaven you are safe. And then, dearest, when I am with you we shall laugh at these and similar fears. You have said we must hope and I do hope and believe. But I *do* wish I could hear from you more frequently. Will you *try*, my love, and let me have a letter, let me see, I will be satisfied to hear *once* a *month*. Is not that *very moderate?* You *said* you would write *once* a *fortnight*, you know, before you left.

I know you have not much leisure. I still hope to hear this week.

It is May fair day (and 'tis raining). Do you remember being at Totnes on this day some four aye *four* years ago? I do, and you came up in the evening and Winnie and you and I walked up the hill. Ah. It was a fine night then. *Now* 'tis gloomy and tearful. I wonder where you will be on this day four years hence? What a vain speculation.

Last Monday week I went to Plymouth with father and Mr. Hains to see Dr. Budes, at least the gentlemen went to the doctor. I did not. I am sorry to tell you he gave him but faint hope. He says it is a gall stone in some pipe, and *nothing* can be done. Nature may wear it out (he had seen such cases) or it might remain and close the pipe entirely. He is to eat and drink all strengthening things, and endeavor to get as strong as he can. That is all that *can* be done, he says. I fear the result much. He is continually wishing Spencer were home, then he says I should have a home. But we should not fear, neither is it well to anticipate evil. I *hope* he will recover.

I wonder, dearest, where you are now, and how you are, how you are looking, and a hundred other things. It seems to me you are away from me such an illimitable distance that I never can see you again, but that is nonsense, is it not? You will not be away from me forever. Hope does, indeed as you say, make the time speed rapidly. You have been gone nearly six months already. Years will soon fly away – and then – we shall meet again. I wonder if we shall be much altered when that time comes. Our *love* will not be. What happiness is in that thought; what a world of thought, and feeling, and joy, and gratitude does that one word *love* contain! My dear, dear George, how I thank you for having called forth those feelings which but for you would have lain dormant, and I should have been ignorant of happiness and of my own heart. Now I know I love and I am happy for *you* love me. Oh in all the sorrow that I have lately known, how much worse would it have been, how hopeless should I have felt and miserable *but* for you, my darling George. And how proud it makes me when I think that he who has my heart is worthy of all the love and even more than I can give him.

I have just sent in to see if there is a letter so I will not close this until the messenger returns. Are my hopes doomed again to disappointment? Yes! Once more, "no letter" is the answer, but I dare say there will be one tomorrow. The mail often arrives on a Thursday.

I shall now, my dearest George, conclude. I answered your last letter in the one I wrote about a month ago. Father & Alicia send their love. And, my beloved, you know you have all the love of your

Little Addey

6 July 1852

21 Down's Buildings
Albany, New York

My own dear Addey,

I'm afraid you will scold me for playing the truant again for I think it is more than a month since I wrote last. I don't know how it is but I cannot make up my mind to sit down and write long letters now like I used to, and I am sure it is not that I think of you less. I think it must be that I love you so much better than formerly and I cannot express my feelings toward you (by letter) as I feel them in my heart. Yes, my dear, that must be the reason. My desire to see & talk to you is so great sometimes that I work myself quite into a rage to think you are so many miles away from me and no chance of seeing you for months & months to come. (I half wish sometimes I had never left England – but I had had a wish to see America for years before I started & my wish has been gratified in this respect & it is wrong now to reject it.) My hope in the future is that I may live to make Addey my wife & end my days in peace & happiness on my native soil a true Briton. I should never wish to forswear my country which every foreigner must do before he can expect to get along "anyways smart" in this great county of freedom & liberty.

I can hardly tell how long I shall remain in this vicinity. It was first intended that I should travel about from one agency to another enlivening up the agents & making 'em do more trade as I went along, but I have been so fortunate (or unfortunate) as to make such a large business in this agency that they cannot easily find a man fitted to take charge of it. You cannot manage men here like in the old country. They are so captious & whimsical – and so little George has to remain here until he can meet with a likely person to help his burden off his shoulders. The fact is, my dear Addey, our manager here (Mr. Roberts) is a very excellent good man and I highly respect him as a man, but he is so careful & cautious (& *slow*) or as Mr. Clarke would say, isn't "springy" enough to keep the trade up to the pitch it ought to be. James Virtue is a first-rate fellow for business when he thinks proper to set his mind to it (but that's too seldom) so you see my dear, that whatever progress I make here must be all by my own efforts with no helping hand and 'tis uphill work I assure you. But then I like it. If I did not have my mind constantly on the work I should be miserable. As it is I am never so jolly as when I am cutting about & polishing up all the fellows I have about me.

In all domestic matters I am a mere cipher. There are several ladies & gentlemen boarding at the same house and strange to say, I never feel so lonely & by myself as when they are all about laughing & chatting & idling their time away. The women here (most that I have seen) are particularly idle & frivolous. They sit about the drawing room in *rocking* chairs & rock away with all their might to the imminent danger of a fellow's toes if he happens to be passing anywhere near them & then they chatter, chatter, scream & laugh more like a parcel of parrots than decent Christian women. I have but one friend here & he is an Englishman named Smallcrass, as good-hearted a little fellow as ever breathed. He formerly belonged to the Mechanic's Institute in London, the same to which Jem Glanville used to belong. He remembered Jem very well, but they were not intimately acquainted. Our rooms are on the same floor & we often pay each other a friendly visit to talk over old times and have a most refreshing bit of private scandal on the American manners & customs.

"What do they drink," you ask. Why the names of their different mixtures would fill a volume. Among the leading ones are "gin sling," "stone fence," "egg nog," "brandy smash," "sherry cobbler," "Tom & Jerry," "mint julep," sarsaparilla, lemonade & etc., etc. Ice creams & sherry cobblers are favorite beverages with the ladies, but upon the whole, I think they are really more temperate in their food & viands than the English. Many never drink anything but ice water for breakfast, dinner & supper. Yes, they have cider here, but *such* cider. I have tasted it *once only*.

Well, my dear, I must get this posted tonight or you will not get it for a week later so good bye, my dear little Addey. I envy my letter. Write soon.

Ever yours,
Geo Little Virtue

Yesterday was a great day here. It was the 4th of July, the anniversary of American Independence & the people have "quite a time."

I have just heard that my poor brother John at the Cape is dead, leaving a wife and child. I have not secured further particulars than this. Farewell, dear Addey, all earthly things must perish but true love will last forever.

George's job in the U.S. was selling the Art Journal, *the most prestigious art periodical of the time. Its engravings included work belonging to Queen Victoria and Prince Albert that had been exhibited at the Crystal Palace Exhibition. James Sprent Virtue, George's cousin and son of the head of the firm, was in charge of the American operation. The journal was published in installments, each issue providing income for the next. It first turned a profit in 1852. Copies are still available in rare book shops.*

BOWDON 13 JULY 1852

My own dearest George,

Another month is gone since I wrote to you last. You have been away more than six months now. Yes, love, you *will* "soon be home again." I wish we were not so far apart, but it is only for a short time so we must not think it wrong. I shall be so glad to see you. It seems to me such a long time since we met. I keep fancying that you will be here soon. It is from your having been down somewhere about this time of the year for two or three years past, but alas! it will not be so this year. And you will be a great stranger when next I see you, though you will hardly be a stranger either, at least not to me. How natural everything in the Old Country will be to you. Everybody and everything will seem to you like an old friend.

There is a perfect mania amongst our young men, and not only the young men, for going to Australia. We are nearly every week hearing of somebody. Alicia says you had better come home "for there will be lots of money to be made when everybody is gone to Australia."

We have had a General Election and on the polling day, Maria and myself went to Mrs. Taylor's and it was such a busy day. Everybody was in a high state of excitement. I was slightly excited myself and was very glad when I found they had elected Mr. Mills, the Liberal member, a new man. I have withdrawn my favor from Mr. Baldwin, the old Conservative member. It passed off quietly, with no rows or fights.

How clearly you state your "withdrawal of your favor" from the conservative candidate, Addey. I almost forgot that women were not allowed to vote until many years later, after a long and hard battle for women's suffrage. I was glad to see they had strong opinions long before they could act on them.

I was so glad, dearest, to receive your last letter. You are so kind and I surely am blessed most highly in your love. I pray that it may never lessen. I must, and do, endeavor to deserve it. May I ever have such a softening, calming influence over your ruffled spirits as you tell me I now have. My darling George, I have said I wished I loved you less, but *now* I do not, for I should not then be worthy of such love as yours.

Wednesday afternoon: We have just received invitations to Maria's wedding tomorrow; that is, we are not going to the church, but we are to be of the party who are to be merry after the bridal pair are gone. When Alicia enquired if Maria was to be married tomorrow, Walter very quietly said, "I must not tell." I think it is quite nonsense to make such an impenetrable secret of it. I daresay there will be a good many tears shed tomorrow, but then, she is only going over to Newton. But it must be very sad for the friends at the home of the bride, the thought of losing her from out of the family, a sort of breaking up and shattering old and familiar habits and associations. I know it will be very lonely and miserable when Alicia goes away. But be assured, I do not regret the prospect of her happiness, for if at any time a feeling of sorrow for my own sake comes over me like a cloud, I chase it hence as altogether selfish and unworthy, and look forward to Compton's arrival for her sake with hope and pleasure. Dear Alicia, she does indeed deserve happiness. She has ever been good and kind and so true to him. What does he not owe to her, for having kept her so long waiting and expecting. Strong indeed is the love of woman. I consider her and Winnie to be patterns of constancy, what say you?

> ➸ *Winnie's happy marriage to Tom must have been encouraging, but Alicia's prolonged engagement may have stirred up anxiety in Addey over her own situation. I hope Spencer did well in the Asian trade and their married life was more comfortable as a result.*

I am very glad to see by your letter that your brother Jim is expected home this summer. I should much like to see him, but I suppose it is hardly likely yet, and Ted, too. I am very glad he is perfectly recovered. I cannot but feel flattered at the very favourable opinion he formed of me. I hope it will never be forfeited.

Alicia is so busy. She rather expects Spencer home next week! But when he wrote last he had not quite decided by what route he would return except that he would not be able to see Winnie nor should he come via New York. He had decided on leaving in May, so that if he comes overland, he will be here next week. Fancy so soon. I cannot realize it at all. It seems to me all nonsense that he should be so near home. I shall not believe it until I see him.

Now, my darling George, I shall say good night. I shall soon have a letter from you again. You don't know what treasures they are to me.

Father, whom I am glad to say, is not worse, though not well, and Alicia, send their love to you, and you know, dearest, you have all of

Your little Addey's

8 AUGUST 1852 ALBANY, NEW YORK

My dear little Addey,

Once more I have the pleasure of writing to my own true & faithful wife. It seemed such a long time since I heard from you that I really was getting anxious and disconcerted about it, but you write just as often as I do myself so I must not find fault on that score.

With your letter last Sunday I received one from Father containing some mournful intelligence. My poor brother John died about Christmas last at Algoa Bay where he had gone for the benefit of his health, but he rapidly got worse and died far away from every friend, and I fear, from every comfort that a dying bed requires. His poor wife & child are gone to live with her uncle who lives in Malmesbury, Cape of Good Hope. Dear old Jack, with all his faults, was a thoroughly good fellow at heart & now he is gone away forever. I can scarcely believe he is really dead sometimes.

Bill has thought proper to try his hand at soldiering once more. He has enlisted in an East India Corps & expects to be drafted off there soon. He writes home perfectly satisfied with what he has done. He is promoted to full corporal already and I daresay in his own quiet way he fully expects to return home a Major General or Grand Commander, at least. Well, I do not care much about this for he doesn't seem to succeed at anything else. Let him go. And poor Ted. Just as he was out of his time, he had his leg break out again and now he is once more laid up – but I hope not for long. The rest of my relations at home are all well & going along as usual.

And so you really expect Spencer Compton home so soon. Why, dear me, I suppose he is with you by this time. Well, he is a "lucky fellow" now. Was it not Spencer who once said "Virtue is a lucky fellow." Oh, no, I think that was Tom Glanville.

Well, they are both happy now, I suppose – and old Virtue must make up his mind to buffet through the world for another year before he can hope to return for dear little Addey. You know I am quite resolved to come home next autumn, even if I have to return – which I expect they will want me to do – and to make up my mind to settle here. I do not quite relish this idea yet although I am more used to American manners & customs now – & do not feel so strange & uncomfortable as I did here at first. Uncle George will be out here soon, and after some talk with him, I daresay I shall make up my mind whether to settle here or in England.

Ah me, it is very warm and close. The glass says 92 degrees in the shade. I must go & cool off with some sacred music on the flute – and some ice water. A great blessing here is the ice water. I don't know how I could live without it.

I wish your Cousin Maria joy with all my heart. I suppose the next marriage I shall have to rejoice over will be sister Alicia's. I say, Addey, wouldn't it be jolly if you & I were going to be married at the same time? Fancy that? Do you know I think I ought not to have let you return back from London last summer, but married you right away & smuggled you off over here. But I had my fears what sort of country I was coming to, and to see you miserable or unhappy through me, I should have gone mad. So perhaps 'tis as well as it is. I feel I have to depend entirely on myself for there is no favor shown to relations in our house and so I am independent – and if only I had little Addey for my wife, a little cottage and a gun, dear me, I should be a happy fellow. As it is now when I leave off work I seem to feel such a sort of vacuity of mind, nothing but such thoughts as these seem to interest me.

I fancy what a pattern you will be to some of the American ladies – flighty, giddy things, that's what they are, haven't got common sense.

Give my love to Father and Alicia and remember me kindly to all who enquire for me.

And so goodbye my dear, good, kind Addey. I wouldn't be without your love for all the dollars in America – and all the American women to boot.

I cannot write such long letters now as I used to, so don't kick up a row about it like a good girl. Give us a kiss.

Adieu,
GLV

17 October 1852

104 State Street
Rochester, New York

My dear little Addey,

It seems such a long time since I wrote you last that I'm afraid you will think I deserve a "blowing up." I received your last letter in New York since which time I have been cutting about like a young sky rocket, not having time to answer your letter before.

Last week I went with James Virtue to Buffalo & Niagara Falls and am now left in this city where I shall remain for the next two months or so. After that I shall resume my post in Albany and hold on there until the spring when uncle will be out. We expected him this fall but it seems as if he will not come so soon.

And so you would like me to return & settle down in my native country, would you? I think it would be better and I am sure you would be happier, which is the greatest consideration to me. I will try & arrange this if I can possibly see my way. You see I have worked myself into something of a position here which I should have to abandon were I to return to the old country where I should have to make a fresh start. There is a sort of rivalry existing between our establishment here and the old country business – and it is a difficult thing to work between the two. Money can be made faster here and more easily but then there are fewer comforts and the climate is more trying than in England. One fact is certain – I should be happy with my own little Addey for a wife anywhere, but then in the event of any reverses of fortune – I cannot bear to think of this, for myself I could rough it through the world with the best, and would incur any hardship rather than my Addey should ever feel the curse of poverty – and this through me. 'Tis a serious thought and it makes me feel the heavy responsibility I have taken upon myself in centering your affection upon me, when you might have been the happy wife of a better man, though more constant & loving to you, he could not be.

The truth has already dawned upon me that I am a "poor man" and to attain anything like a respectable position in life (or such a position as I would wish to be in when I call you my wife) I must drudge and toil hard for years to come. I know your generous heart will be dictated by love to say you would share my lot with mine, however humble it might be – and the thought of this makes my heart glad – but my own pride is not sufficiently humbled yet to admit of this thought. What time will reduce it to, God knows. It has received some heavy blows the last few years. The world is a book which I have only commenced learning to read & the more I read, the less I like it. But I am tiring you with all this tirade of ill humour so I will change the theme, if you please.

When you go to London, do not fail to call and see my sister. She is a good girl at heart and I think you will like her and I am sure she will be pleased with you. Her address is Mrs. Lawrence, 10 College Place, Camden Town. I shall write to her by this post so she will expect you. I had a letter from her a few days since. She was then in Scotland but expected to be home in about a month. I should like you two to be friends very much – and I think you will be.

Give my kind love to Alicia & Spencer Compton. I hope they are both well. To the Governor also. I hope he is better. And accept the heartfelt devotion of

Yours ever & ever,
Geo L. Virtue

I still intend to come home next Autumn. Will you be willing then to marry a poor man loving you much & with two hands to work – & all I can offer?

George is struggling to come to grips with this adventure of his. He is beginning to appreciate what succeeding in business involves, and is overwhelmed by what he must do to achieve it.

1853

There is a rebellious feeling in my heart

Only four letters survive from 1853, the second year George is in the U.S.: three from George and one from Addey. The letters are considerably longer and more anguished. The increased distance and intervening time between their being written and arriving cause misunderstanding and frustration for both of them. They are hurt by what each interprets as a lack of trust and faith in the other. The harsh exigencies of living and loving on different continents have taken a toll. The letters carry the full weight of their emotions, which they convey to one another with no holds barred.

14 FEBRUARY 1853 ALBANY, NEW YORK
VALENTINE'S DAY

My darling little Addey,

Once more back to my old quarters for which I am very glad, the more so because I can spare the more time to write a long letter to my good little wife.

I was so glad to get your last letter. You had kept me waiting for some little time for it so that I began to grow uncomfortable in my mind. I expected you were in London, but I did not think you had called on my sister. You are both good girls, she for writing & you for calling on her. What a pity that in my impatience I should have suspected her of any unkindness. She is a good girl, but like myself, somewhat wayward at times.

So you vain little soul, you want me to tell you what she says about you. Who could see you without liking you, and if Harriet is at all like her brother, can she help saying you are the darlingest little creature on earth. She will & must say so, but then she has not written to me yet. Non-attention to correspondents is a weakness in our family, I think, and I am the best of the whole of them in this respect. I have written some two or three letters & have had never an answer to any of 'em. They always expect two or three for one of theirs which if they don't get – look out for squalls. Nobody has been so punctual in writing as my little Addey & while she is true & constant, what do I care for anything? Not a jot.

Tuesday, 11 p.m. "I must go up stairs & finish my letter to my little wife." Thus spake your humble servant a few minutes ago to Mr. Hovey with whom I have just been playing cribbage & he has beaten me too, of course. Well, "vive la bagatelle." I have plenty to occupy my mind & yet I feel a poor lonely old bachelor, but I shall not be so always if I'm a good boy. Addey, your letters always seem to inspire me with new life & hope. How dear a thing it is to have a woman's love. What would this life be without it.

To me the absence of your love would make my future life a perfect blank. What's the use of eternally counting dollars & cents which seems the ultimatum of my existence at present. Addey, when we are married you will have to learn me to be economical. I cannot save money. I have been over here a year now & am scarcely better off than when I started. True, I have had to travel about a good deal & the extra expenses of this I have had to meet myself ('twas always allowed me in the old country). However, I am settled down to this agency now where I shall remain as long as I like and I am quite *determined* to save money now. See if I will not. I cannot make a fortune at one leap as I once used to think, but I can earn sufficient to make us both happy & comfortable. My vaulting ambition gets the better of my judgement sometimes, but this latter idea has been latent in my mind always. If I do not become a great man, you will be the means of making me a good man & this is all we should aspire to.

I feel sure I could make money faster if they would have let me start for myself, but this they would not agree to, so until I can see my way clearer, I must consent to remain a servant while I continue in this business. I think after we are married, my dear, & we save up a little money, we will go out to Australia. How would you like to go there?

I am very sorry to learn poor Alicia does not enjoy her usual health. Give my best love to her & Compton & to sister Winnie & Tom & the little ones when you write.

I have every reason to hope I can come home this year if I like, but whether it would not be wiser to wait to remain until the following spring, time will prove. Were you saying once that it would be better to wait four years until Winnie came home before we married? I don't see the force of this argument, my dear, I must confess, but I should be the last in the world to wish you to leave England while your father wished you to remain & it was your own inclination as well. I think I shall be able to remain in London if I try, but whether I shall decide upon doing this will altogether depend upon circumstances, which at present I cannot at all foresee.

I am very glad you have become acquainted with Harriet, & trust you two will be always good friends. It is for myself to prove some day a true husband and a dutiful brother. Frank & Harry are jolly little fellows, are they not, and Fanny is a dear little doll. I am sure they will be very fond of their Aunty. I should have much preferred introducing you to all my friends & relations myself but this I have been unable to do. Father you will like, I am sure. He is one of the right mold, but too kind & indulgent.

Well, my dear little Addey, I must say goodbye once more. It is getting late & I must be up early in the morning as I am going out of town & to be candid, my eyelids are beginning to complain. So let us kiss & say good night. Write me a good long letter, love to everybody. Be a good girl & always believe in the constant love

Of yours forever & aye,
G Little Virtue

Just before I left London Aunt Virtue was making me bashful by asking all about you – but from my replies she cannot but have formed a favorable impression. I wonder what Uncle will say when I tell him I think of getting married. "Eh? Get married? What do ye think ye are going to do with a wife & can hardly keep yourself?" But when this time comes I shall be in a position to talk down all such prejudices.

> ➢ *All seems relatively well in this first letter. And then: Addey has written George a letter, one among the missing (perhaps just as well), to which he responds vehemently.*

11 April 1853

21 Down's Building
Albany, New York

My dear Addey,

A foretaste of "curtain lectures" was your last, my dear, & I like you none the less for speaking your mind so freely. 'Twas plain common sense, practical though severe – true, but cutting. With my many failings, how could I expect you would forever look over my faults. You act wisely to chide me now for it might come too late hereafter.

I am but a poor man placed in a position where too strict an economy would overthrow me. Instead of saving pennies I have used all my energy to create a firm business around me & it is a satisfaction for me to feel that I have succeeded in this. Were the business mine own, I would show you, Addey, that I could make money. I can make it now for my masters. Perhaps someday I may make it for myself, but you may only look upon me now in the light of a journeyman earning a steady salary. Since I have been in this country I have not been idle nor dissolute, nor a spendthrift – but have kept on in a steady track, exerting all my time to increasing the business not for myself but for my employers. My dear Addey, if you but knew all I have endured & contended with since I left England you would not judge me so harshly – no, not that for you have every reason to say what you did, but you would judge me by my endeavors as a whole.

Let us be plain. I beg you to think well over what I now write. Would your life really be happier to share your fate with me & my many failings? Look about you & see how many more there are who would make you a more comfortable home. If you have sad thoughts & forebodings before they exist – realities must be worse. You have made a wrong selection. Choose again before it is too late. I would not marry you (much as I love you) to make your future life miserable, for all the world. For my own part, I do not look upon this life as being of so much importance; better to have trials & adversities occasionally or there would be those who would wish to be tied to this earth forever. To die after a well-spent life is the best rest I know of & the only great end worth looking forward to with so much anxiety.

Health is better than wealth & contentment the greatest happiness but all of these are small matters compared with the great end. Your heart has governed your head hitherto – & now as you grow older & wiser your head masters your heart & you see as folly what you formerly felt with affection.

You say you still love me dearly & I like to believe you – but your better judgment comes to the rescue. Now what before was your whole existence is dwindled down to but a small part of what it once was & you could easily overcome it altogether should occasion demand it. Let is be so if it will make you happier. Think of me only as something gone by, a day dream, a toy, treasured once but now thrown aside for more important realities. Your happiness is more to me than all besides. Therefore, in seeking to do that for yourself which will prove best hereafter, consult your own free will entirely & do as your good common sense dictates without regard to any engagement you have made with me. Let that be a minor consideration. Think of me sometimes but only as a poor fellow who would be unable to make you as happy or comfortable a home as you would desire.

After all I really think I am most unkind in writing to you in this manner – although I feel like it. Your last letter was written under depressing circumstances – your poor father lying on a bed of sickness from which God grant he may soon recover & that perfect feeling of loneliness you must necessarily feel in consequence. Ought I not to make great allowances for this & try to cheer you up with words of sympathy & tenderness instead of rambling over the dark passages of my inmost thoughts. I love you very dearly, Addey, & I wish I could be with you now. I often dream of meeting you.

The management of this agency requires nearly all my time & thought & the possibility of leaving it for any length of time – so far as I can see – would only loosen from me the burthen of a dependent's situation, to be once more thrown on my own resources. I am yet strong & young, & although I cannot anticipate, I look forward with hope to the future.

Believe me, dear Addey,
Ever Yours Affectionately,
Geo Little Virtue

Kind love to all

I had a few dollars saved up & a thief broke into my office & stole them from me – the same morning I received your letter. "Save," says Addey. Yes! Save to be robbed, thought GLV. I don't think I was very amiable that day. Such is life.

I have some idea that Uncle is extending the business to Australia. This will be a fine chance for me if he thinks I am "baked" sufficiently hard. My birthday tomorrow, 25. How soon the sands of life run out. Be happy, Addey, dear, & always act & think for the best. 'Tis no use being miserable.

> *Poor George. He feels wounded by what Addey has written, but defends himself, outlining his travails. No more dreams now of making a fortune quickly and returning to marry his beloved. He is committed to the challenge of succeeding and has begun to realize what this entails. He tells her she must decide her fate. I am touched by how concerned he is about earning enough to make her comfortable.*
>
> *The letter ends on an upbeat note. Bravo, George.*

29 April 1853 Bowdon

My dearest George,

Your letter arrived yesterday, and although I know this cannot go out of England for a week, I am constrained to answer it at once. Oh what would I not give if you were but here, that I might talk to you, that I might *tell* you how much you have wronged me, how deeply you have wounded me. I can hardly tell why I wrote that letter that has caused all this misery.

I felt there was a possibility of its being misunderstood as soon as it was gone, but I hoped it would not be. I believed I was safe. This letter received yesterday proves that I was *not*, that you think me mercenary and heartless. I confess I was wrong. I had no *right* to say so much as I did. I now ask you to forgive me and I promise never again to proffer counsel in any way to you unasked.

But George, dearest, you have no right to judge so bitterly of me. I fondly dreamed your love would plead for me, but I find your *pride* is stronger. You say "there are those who would wish to be tied to this earth forever," but I desire that you count not *me* amongst those. You have said some cutting things and there is a rebellious feeling in my heart – my pride – for I am not without it – struggling with that love which is my life, for although you think it has "dwindled down to a small part of what it *was*," I feel that it has never had a firmer hold on me, that it was never so strong, so absorbing, so confiding as now. I have loved you for years.

There *was* a time when I could have "easily overcome" it, but *now*, George, if you bid me forget our engagement, you take from me my only hope, all that I have to live for. Then I should be indeed *alone*. It has formed the silver lining to the dark cloud that lowers over my days.

For sad thoughts and forebodings, in whom do they not exist *sometimes*? You yourself have them, and at times of sorrow and tears, they *will* make themselves felt. When I wrote you *that* letter, I was in daily fear of beholding a beloved father die. He has indeed been on the verge of the dark grave, but I thank God the danger is past and now we have hopes of his recovery. Picture me thus in grief and mourning (and I *have* known sorrow, George, since you saw me and I have wept tears that have left their traces on my heart) and then tell me if you find it in your heart to say, "I love you as well as ever"? Oh, if I could read forgiveness and love from your eyes, and take its assurance from your lips, I should be happy indeed. But I know you do love me. You will not tell me to think of you as a "day dream." You have been and are to me a bright and loving day dream, and if you take from me my happy dream, you will leave me prostrate and aimless.

Think of me then, not prejudiced against me, but of your own Addey, whose whole sum of happiness, whose only hope in life is derived from your abiding love. "Choose again?" Do you not believe, George, that I would more willingly share your fate, even were it a beggar's, than become wife to the proudest of the land? Believe me, it is so.

I shall not close this letter yet, but now that I have relieved myself of the burden of unhappiness that has lain so heavily on my heart since reading yours, I shall feel more at ease.

Wednesday evening

I would that I could search your heart now. Could it give me peace or make me unhappy? I flatter myself you cannot be angry with me. Still it gives me more pain to know that you are dissatisfied with me *now* than it used to do. Is this a proof that my love is less strong? I think not. Pray, dearest, dismiss this idea from your head, for I will not believe it has existence in your *heart*. Once more I say forgive me. I could not ask this if I did not love you. I never dreamed of your being either "idle, dissolute, or a spendthrift." Believe me, dearest, I could not have the feeling of love, and pride, and *respect* for you which I ever have had if it had been so. I know you, George, at least I like to think I do, and I know you deserve all the love that is in my woman's heart. And you know you have it.

I am afraid I have said too much. I would not for all the world lose your love and, may I add, *respect*. Know me better and do not, oh! *do not doubt my love*. It is worse now than if you were even in London. It is so long before I can know if you still permit me to think of you as my own George. I wish your next letter was come, but will fret no more but hope.

I am glad to tell you that my dear father is much better – and now that the peril is past, the doctor gives us every reason to hope that he will be a strong man again yet. Who would have thought it – not the doctor. One day three weeks ago, he said when he left he did not expect to see him again. He did not think he *could* live twenty-four hours, and *now* he is able to go out of doors.

Alicia and her little son are getting on capitally. I am going up to see them as soon as Father gets well. She and Spencer desire their love to you and so does Father.

Dearest George, write as soon as you can and believe me, *I cannot be happy unless I am*

Your own Addey

She is contrite, realizing her sharp words have met their mark. George questions whether she has made a wise choice and tells her she must decide.

She tries to explain her state of mind and asks for his forgiveness, realizing how badly she has hurt him. How bravely they lay out their grievances. I can feel the barbs in the pit of my stomach. Both are stinging from the rebukes of the other. How close did they come to a breakup? Perhaps their courage in expressing their worst fears was a means of dealing with them.

The next letter is dated six months after the two that were fraught with such anguish. The lovers have rekindled their trust in and affection for one another, presumably in letters that have not survived.

23 November 1853

121 Willoughby Street
Long Island

Now my little darling,

I must answer your two last dear kind letters. I am afraid you will be impatient with me for not writing sooner, and be thinking all sorts of dreadfully unpleasant things as a reason for my silence; but this time happily I can excuse myself on good grounds, namely that I have been waiting until James Virtue returned in order that I might have something tangible to talk to you about, and now that he has returned and matters have been arranged more satisfactorily, I hasten to write to my darling little wife & to tell her that my mind is free or partly so, which is saying a great deal more than I ever could say before, since I have been out in this Land of Freedom(?) & Liberty(?).

I had a long argument with Master James, the subject being Labour versus Capital, & it has ended so far in my favour, that my future services shall be considered nearly equivalent to his money (or rather his father's money) in the working of the business. So I only have to keep at it close – to put myself on an equality with him or with anyone in this free country. I have been perpetually working with a sort of mist before my eyes but now my future is clear before me & you shall see, my dear, that I can make myself worthy of your love which I prize above all earthly things.

I have made up my mind to settle in New York at any rate for a few years until we get better off & then we can see what will be best. In the meantime I must see about making arrangements for your coming out here. James Virtue was talking with me about it this morning. He thinks the best way would be for you to come out with Mrs. Roberts & Miss Ridgeway and if you would consent to this, he has left word at home for some of his family (his sister or his father or mother) to go down to Devonshire & plan with you so that you would be as well cared for as if I were with you.

Now what does Addey say to all this? It is very kind of James, is it not, and it makes me feel not a little proud that they take so much interest in our welfare. But you see, Addey, I want to come home myself and fetch you, to be married in England. I may not see England for many years & this would be as good an opportunity as any. You see what a selfish old fellow I am – but I know you are kind & considerate & can feel in your mind what my thoughts are. I think you know me as well as anybody in this world, almost even better than I know myself, I think sometimes. You see, Addey, they don't want me to leave here & they will prevent it I know if they can. They would do well for me but it must be a secondary consideration, they study their own interest or the interest of the business first (which is right perhaps) but, hang it, a fellow may do as he likes for once in his life – and I want to go home next fall to marry Addey, see my friends once more & then return. It will be a jolly, jolly dreadful shame if I cannot do so. Hang the business. It has so bent & twisted & bridled my mind that I had begun to doubt if I really had a mind at all, but I feel now as I write that I have & they must give way to me in this or I shall bolt the traces. James is a good fellow. I like him very much. He is practical in his ideas, too, far more so than I am. He argues that what it would cost for me to go home & fetch you would go far toward furnishing a house, "cradles & so on, you know."

The greatest wish of my heart is to make Addey my wife – my next to come home & fetch her. So my dear little son, can you offer me any advice in my predicament? Your letters always come like a gleam of sunshine on my mind which hitherto has been too full of ill forebodings – but the mist is clearing away now, as I said before, and I see in the future many years of happiness & prosperity. The shackles of trade have tended to tame my sometimes too wild spirit and I believe after all I shall make you a decent sort of a husband.

In your last letter you complain of ill health. I hope you are quite recovered, my dear. Just do take the greatest care of yourself. In this country the climate is so trying that a most hardy constitution is requisite to bear up against the two extremes of heat & cold, so you will do all in your power to keep well & hearty. I feel quite well & jolly & although I am upstairs in my room without a fire, I am writing to you & that keeps me warm enough. I cannot bear to sit in a room with a nasty black stove – but in this very cold weather, they can scarcely be done without.

Why, here's the end of two sheets – but I won't *count the words* this time. Oh for the happy days of yore. I love to think back upon them.

Thank you for the violets. They did indeed remind me of Bowdon.

Well, now, Addey, you mustn't keep a fellow chattering here all night. Let me go. I dreamt of you last night. I thought you looked prettier than ever. You are a little darling, Addey, and I love you very much. Kiss me then. Oh you young wretch, you have bitten my neck.

Give my love to Father Watson. You know, Addey, we are both young & hearty. If you like, after we have been married a little while & got matters a little settled, I don't see at all why your father couldn't come over & live with us. We should only have to work a little harder & that we would cheerfully do. Oh, I do believe we will accomplish much good when we get settled. I wish we were now for my mind will never know rest until we are united.

Next Thursday is Thanksgiving – a day devoted by the Americans to eating and praying. I have written to Shallcross to come down. If he does we shall take a walk to Fort Hamilton & back, a small go, only 18 miles. Shall is very fond of walking. We used in Rochester to talk of walking all the way from Liverpool to London when we go home – too romantic an idea though to be carried out in this practical age of railroads & ships.

I have not sealed my letter but I must do so tonight before I turn in for I shall have to be up early tomorrow in order to have it posted in time for tomorrow's mail which will leave at 12 noon.

I have been to a lecture this evening, the subject was, let me see, "Books & Reading," delivered at the Brooklyn Institute by a clever little humpbacked Irishman named Giles. I never talk to you about the news of the day because I daresay you know better about the state of affairs than myself, but when we get settled, we must converse freely upon this as well as on all other topics.

Oh, how I long for a true friend and companion. My heart yearns for you, Addey, more & more every day. Never fear that my love for you will or can ever lessen. In the hurry & turmoil of business, your presence may for a time be obscured from my mind but only for a time to be renewed again stronger & dearer than ever. Make up your mind to be in America this time next year. Either I shall come & fetch you or you will come out to me with Mrs. Roberts. I *want* to come & fetch you and I will try my hardest to do so. Anyway we have both waited too long. I only half exist until you are with me. My love for you teaches me that you would wait for me all through this life in the hope that we should be united in the world to come for I cannot believe love such as ours will cease upon this earth.

Kind love to all, dear Addey.
Ever yours
GLV

George would like to have a share in the business instead of being only an employee. He is competitive with James, the son of the boss, who has the advantage. However, it is clear he is not about to give up on the venture. He has begun to feel more confident.

Did Addey's father ever consider coming to live with them? It was so like George to suggest it.

1854

Your portrait looks more Yankee than I like

This year is the third of George's time in the U.S. and the seventh of George and Addey's courtship. Only four letters survive: three from George and one from Addey. Much of the writing concerns deciding on a plan for Addey to join her beloved. Both have endured frustration, loneliness, longing, and despair during their extended separation.

Addey has left Bowdon and Totnes to live with her (finally) now-married sister Alicia at Prospect Villa in Peckham Rye in South London. She is enjoying herself going to the theatre and partaking of other cultural offerings, but is uncomfortable with not knowing when she will leave England. The main obstacle is George's inability to save money. It is clear in the letters that each misunderstands the other, but they convey strongly what they are experiencing without rancor. Each of them retains a concern for the well-being of the other in spite of their own grievances.

Was George's failure to save money due to his youth, his being paid very little, or his nature? Or was it the instability of his life in those early days? Given this early history, it is remarkable he was able to provide well for a large family and become a pillar of society – as he did. Did he need the steadying influence of Addey, as he tells her so often, acknowledging how essential she is to him? This is of course one of his most endearing traits.

9 JANUARY 1854 26 JOHN STREET, NEW YORK

My dear little Addey,

I have received two letters from you and I must see about answering right away. By the way, I did not know I had kept you waiting for a letter so long – six weeks. However, I can only promise to be a better boy in the future.

How I should like to be able to say for certain that I could come home & fetch you in the fall, but I much doubt, my dear Addey, if I shall be able to do so, looking the matter over carefully & apart from my own private wishes. I cannot help thinking that it will be the best way for you to come out in the spring with Mrs. Roberts & Miss Ridgeway. If I cannot come & fetch you I shall take special care to make every arrangement for your comfort & happiness. Mrs. Roberts is a good pious soul in her way & Miss Ridgeway is a clever, good-tempered, amiable little girl & therefore I have no doubt you will spend a pleasant time on your passage out. It seems a great pity that I cannot come & fetch you, the disappointment is greater to me than it can possibly be to you, my dear Addey, for it is what I had set my mind upon from the time when I left England now more than two years ago. I had big hopes for the future then & so I have now but they are almost dormant. The fact is you must come out here, Addey. I miss you more & more every month. How pleasant it would be to have you here, to see you every day & talk over old times & lay out our plans together for the future for you must understand that it is far from my thoughts to remain but here all our lifetimes.

Even as it is now I think I could return to London if I very much wished to do so – & sometimes I have half a mind that way, but with all the pros & cons, the fact is as I said before, you must make up your mind to come out in the spring. You have already waited far too long for me, and I can only feel half like myself until we are united.

I do not know exactly the time Mrs. Roberts has arranged for leaving England but I think she told me before she left here that she would return somewhere about the latter end of April or the early part of May, but in my next I shall be able to furnish you with more particulars. *I am greatly disappointed & sorely vexed* that I cannot come home & fetch you, the more so when I feel that I *could* have done so had I been allowed to exercise more of my *own* will in the matter, but it is no use growling; every dog will have his day & mine will come some day so I hope.

My kind love to your father & believe me,
dear Addey,
Ever yours,
G.L.V.

I will promise to write again in a week or ten days time. Do not say good bye forever to your friends because I hope you will see them all again in a year or two after you leave. I am half afraid they will make so much fuss that you will be unable to leave. Does that smack of jealousy? I'm afraid it does. My greatest pride is that you have never given me cause for jealousy & my best hope is in the full confidence that you never will.

The stove is gone out & my fingers are freezing. So good night, little lady. Take care of yourself. Give my love to Alicia & Winnie when you write to them. Say I am rather elated with the idea of so soon making little Addey Mrs. Virtue.

Talking about getting married, I must tell you, on New Year's day, I was in Albany & called on a young fellow who used to board at the same house I did. He was married about twelve months ago & now he has a *baby* – a real boy. His wife was sick abed upstairs. He was sitting down by the stove in his shirt sleeves (always a token of discomfort to my mind). The fact of having one little one was very well but where would it end? Fancy one or so a year for about twenty years. George, for shame, how dare you talk so to me? 'Twas was only a passing thought on the future.

Good night,

George and Addey did have six children who survived, three boys and three girls, and two who did not. The second surviving son, Herbert, was, as I have mentioned, my grandfather, to whom I was devoted. He was not unlike his father: warm, kind, bright, with a good sense of humor, and not primarily business-oriented.

My mother, his daughter Isobel, would say that he never rushed to get the train in the morning, saying there would be another along anon.

23 APRIL 1854, SUNDAY MORNING BROOKLYN, NEW YORK

My dear Addey,

I must make up my mind to sit down and write to you at some length and endeavor to explain to you our position in order that your mind may be more at rest, for I can easily understand by your last

Diane's mother Isobel with her parents, Herbert and Edith.

letter the unpleasant state of mind you are placed in owing to the unsettled way in which I seem to you to be planning out our future, but in my love for you, I am not "wavering" & when people tell you so, you ought to know me well enough to contradict them.

To come home next June, get married, & return to America, is the great wish of my heart, and always has been since I have been out here. But how to accomplish it is the difficulty that keeps me from "having a mind of my own." You told me once that "money was power." I quite believe you & in my case, it is mind also for if I have not the money I cannot make my mind apparent. You ask me to speak to you plainly & to say exactly what I mean. (Just as if I ever could say anything to Addey that I did not mean.)

By next June, with a little generalship, I might make myself a *fortune* of £100 with a permanent situation out here worth $800 – or over £150 per annum. Do you think that we two could get along on this – for if you do not, then there is the end of the affair, and I shall have to live a miserable old bachelor all the days of my life – for if I did not marry you, I do not think I should ever marry.

For me to come home in June, you see, would swamp all the £100 & it would be a near thing then for us to get out here – and then we would have to go into boarding until we saved enough money to furnish half a house or a small cottage some little distance away from business. But in favor of this would be the satisfaction of my coming to England once more, *our being married there*, & the pleasure of being escort or consort to your ladyship across the Atlantic. This I take it is most to both our liking & is in fact the sunny side of the question. Now let us look at the more sober & economical way.

Could you be prevailed upon to come out alone, the expense would be nearly two thirds less & with the saving, I should be able to get a nice little place & have it fixed up for you by the time you arrive & further, Roberts, who strongly advocates this course of proceeding (the more so, of course, because their interests would not improve by my being away) & he says that you could stay at his house with Mrs. Roberts & his niece until the marriage business was all over and we could be together. James Virtue also thinks this would be the best way and says his folks would be happy to assist in seeing you comfortably shipped and all that sort of thing. There is a new partner in the concern here, Mr. Hemens, & he is now in England settling his affairs there preparatory to his coming out here for good. Now, you might come over very nicely with his family. I do not know them but James Virtue says Mrs. Hemens is a good and lady-like person. They will leave early in this summer. There now, I think I have given you a very lucid statement of how matters are at present, and I shall leave it with you to decide upon which of these two courses we shall form our plans. As far as my own wishes are concerned, I certainly would much rather come & fetch you & chance all other contingencies, but whether this would be the wiser policy remains a question which you yourself must solve. If I had more money, there would be no need for a thought different from my coming home to fetch you. You must think the matter over well, and whichever way you decide upon, I will endeavor to carry out.

The partnership I spoke of once before is too nominal altogether to be termed a reality. It would better serve my purpose to remain an ally until I am better off. I wrote to Uncle as I told you but have received no answer directly or indirectly. I sent the letter home by Mr. Hemans & something strikes me it was not delivered. Time will prove this as it does most things. If I could see Uncle & talk to him a bit, I am sure affairs would assume a different aspect. He is a kind-hearted & good man, I believe, but he is too far away from me in more than one sense.

Give my love to all the folks & as soon as you have made up your mind, sit down & write me your determination. You say I must write oftener. I will do so, but if you please, you have only written me two letters in return for 3 or 4 I have sent you.

Your ever & ever,
G.L.V.

Give my love to Alicia. Talk over our affairs with her, Addey. She is a good sensible girl & her advice should be heeded, but whatever your resolution may be – let it be your wish also for that is to be thought of most of all. I do not care a single pin what people may say or think of me, just so that your faith in me is unshaken.

The weather today is beautiful. The ladies are promenading Broadway thick as bees. Oh you should see Broadway. There is no place like it in England that I have seen, but you will see it soon.

I shall be anxiously waiting for your reply – for I am resolved to be guided by your determination. This will leave tomorrow, the 26th of April – & if you write by return mail, I shall receive it before the 24th of May.

4 August 1854 Prospect Villa

My dearest George,

I dare say you are thinking you ought to have had a letter from me at least a week ago. But I deferred writing until this week that I might have something more to tell you.

Last Sunday I dined with Mrs. Lawrence where I met Edward. They are very well and send their love to you. Your sister says you do not write to her but I think she will write soon. Mrs. Lawrence has seen Mr. Shallcrass who has made a decided impression on her, though I think not a *very* favorable one. I should fancy from her description of him that he must be dreadfully American. She says she would find you just as much so but I hope not. Yet your portrait looks much more Yankee than I like. I think it is not nearly so good as the one I had before. I do not think the mustache at all an improvement, and pray do not continue to wear your *collar turned down.* So much for personal appearances. I think you are not altered otherwise, but then this cannot be like you – much – it is a very ugly likeness. I am much obliged to you for sending it to me, and thank you for thinking of me and getting it done.

On Monday, Mrs. Lawrence and I called on Mrs. Virtue at Ivy Lane but were too late to see her, so we said we would call on the following day at twelve, and then we went to see your Uncle James where we stayed for tea. They were very kind indeed to me and invited me to come again which of course I shall do. Your cousin Ellen thinks you and I are much alike. I shall meet your brother Tom at their house. He has enlisted in the Life Guards. Do you know this? He was very uncomfortable at home, poor fellow. I am sorry he is not to go abroad. Ted sees him often. They say he is *taller* than Edward and very handsome.

I remained at Camden Town on Monday night and Tuesday we went again to Ivy Lane for your sister was very anxious that I should see your aunt. She received me very kindly indeed and took us with her to Finsbury Square directly where we dined and stayed until eight o'clock. They all were very kind. I saw your cousin James there. He is not a bit like I fancied. He was going to call on me, he said. You need not be afraid of my falling in love with him.

Your aunt very much regretted my not going out with Mrs. Roberts. She professed to be interested in us and says she shall be very glad indeed when we are married. Mrs. Roberts promised her that she would receive me at her house and that everything should be satisfactorily arranged and that she would not part with me until I am Mrs. Virtue. She said I am sure she will do all this and will be quite as a mother to you, my dear. She gave me some good advice and when we came away, asked me to come again whenever I liked. They would always be very glad to see me and Mrs. Lawrence too. I think it likely they will be on a more friendly footing in future.

Now about my coming out, I do not know what to say about it. I wish I had known before that you would rather defer it until the spring, and I would have been still at Bowdon, but you spoke so decidedly of this summer or autumn, and argued it so much that I thought you meant it, or, at least, that you were more prepared for me. You know, George, when you wrote to ask me to decide about your coming home, you said it would cost you £100, and that if you did not come home, *that* sum would go far towards preparing a house for us. I understood you had this sum by you. *Now*, you say, by the middle of September – "if nothing unforeseen occurs to prevent" you will have about £20. I could not have mistaken what you said, but it seems rather mysterious that this should have become reduced to so small a sum. Of course, dear George, I do not doubt you in any way, and perhaps I have no right to say anything about it, but it does seem rather unaccountable.

I suppose I had better not come to you until next year – if then. Of course, I feel rather under an obligation, remaining here with Alicia. I know I shall be very welcome to stay as long as I like, yet if I had known *exactly* how you were situated and what you wished, we would not have left Bowdon for a few months. However, it is too late now to regret that.

I have no objection to waiting until spring whatever, *if you* are sure you will be more ready for me then than now. I do not wish to hurry you, but you know I am not situated the same as I was a few months ago while I was at *home*. I could have staid months or years, but now it is different, I am only a visitor. I should not feel comfortable to stay *very* many months. I could not feel independent, you know. You know what I mean. You must decide for me now. I shall not doubt your love for me, dearest; I know it is only your great love for me which leads you to be fearful of hastening our marriage. You fear you will not make me happy and comfortable, but my own George, you know that your love is more than all else to me and to be with you is all I wish. We shall be happy, dearest, if we have to live quietly and economically. Our wants will not be *very* great. I am afraid sometimes you think I care more for my *comfort* than for your love. If ever you do think so, you do me great wrong. Believe it is not so.

But George, I would not come until you wish me, if it be not for a year or two. I am very jolly and enjoying myself very much. Last night we went to the Olympia to hear Robson sing Vilikins. I wish you could hear him. We heard it before at Vauxhall but it was nothing to Robson although we thought that very good. Since I have been here we have been to the two places above named, and to Crenorne and Hampton Court, and to Barnet where Father is now. He is quite recovered and very jolly and sends his love to you, and so do Alicia and Spencer and Mrs. Lawrence and Ted. What a nice fellow he is. I like him very much. So does his cousin Bessie, as Harriet thinks, but he does not care anything about her more than a cousinly regard.

Now my dearest George, I must conclude this long letter. You must write to me directly you receive this, won't you?

Harriet is very anxious for me to go to you as soon as I can, but I think since you wish it, I would rather stay here till next spring. But you must decide finally for me as soon as you get this.

Good bye dearest. Write as soon as you get this. Believe me your own

Addey

Addey's one surviving letter for the year handily and gently expresses her exasperation with George. Her remarks about the portrait he has sent her set the tone: she dislikes his mustache and the state of his collar. (Evidently, collars were worn up before they came down.) And after declaring the picture a "very ugly likeness," she does thank him for it.

Once again she does not hesitate to present herself as an assertive and strong young woman, taking her lover to task for what could, in her mind, be improved upon. And her final statement after a discussion of George's finances, "Of course, dear George, I do not doubt you in any way, and perhaps I have no right to say anything about it, but it does seem rather unaccountable."

14 November 1854 Brooklyn, Long Island

My dear Addey,

Many thanks for your last letter, which I hasten to answer by the return mail.

Although you are still very much displeased with me, I can perceive there is a touch of your old affection left & I must make haste & make peace with you before it all dies out. Of course, I had made up my mind (before receiving your last) that you had quite given me up and had set your mind on someone more worthy of your love, & to be quite candid (as that is to be the order of things) even now I have occasional slight misgivings of that ilk.

I don't know how it is but I cannot talk to you now like I used to. You are so prone to take me up on words & sentences which by being held up & detached from the spirit in which the whole letter was written, give quite a different aspect to my thoughts or to the true state of my feelings as I would have you understand them. I love you Addey as strongly as ever I did – but sometimes I am so strangely & widely misunderstood by you that I often wonder what sympathy there is existing between us, or if in reality there is any. No, I don't mean that either. This is the solution, I think. You estimate my worth by my acts, & they to you must appear so small & insignificant that you seem to be quite led away by this conviction & will not think upon me as really having a soul or spirit beyond those external appearances. If I were only a rich man, I could illustrate better my real mind toward you. Ever since I have been in this business I have experienced nothing but trials, mortifications & disappointments. It is almost too late to choose another occupation, but dear Addey, if you will only continue to love me & believe in me, I will promise to be ever kind & gentle to you. You have all my best thoughts & now if you wish to cast me off, I shall be like a ship at sea without helm or compass & soon shall be wrecked.

I think I told you before that when I took the little cottage, I thought it possible you would come out this fall, but I judged by your letters how much more comfortable & happy you must be with your sister in London that for me to urge you to come out to me while my resources were so limited – I could not make up my mind to do it. I would sometimes look around at the bare walls & scanty furniture & wonder to myself how would Addey like this change. To me in her kindness of heart, she would endeavour to appear contented & happy, but the contrast of what she had or might have been & what she was, the wife of a poor clerk. Oh, but this is all nonsense, Addey. Do be a good, kind girl & like yourself, write to me oftener. You cannot think how grateful I feel every time I hear from you, but don't blow me up so. Is it come to this that I must beg & pray for Addey's love &

sympathy. It seemed to me to be a most unnatural thing to talk about breaking engagements & all that. Do you wish it? I cannot believe you do – it seems so strange & cold. I dislike to think or talk of it. On most other subjects, if I am not wise, I am at least rational, but here I am quite astray. If you have chosen another, I give up all claim, most certainly, if you desire it. You needn't write again – yes, just a line to say you are engaged to another.

Common sense has just prompted me to finish this tomorrow, for I am involving myself in a maze of difficulty & trouble from which I see no escape – so good night, Addey. Will you give us a kiss at parting – only one good night, dearest?

I think I told you in my last that I had given up the cottage. I am now boarding in High Street, Brooklyn, with Captain Gerard. I am very comfortable there. I shall soon be on good terms with you again & and then I shall go ahead once more. I wish you were here. Is it too late for you to come out this year? Whenever I talk reasonably with you, you say I am cold-hearted & unfeeling. I can be happy only under the conviction that you still love me & with this assurance from you I am well prepared to do much this winter, that I shall be more fully prepared to receive you when you have made up your mind to come out. Look on me & my acts with more favor and you will yet find I am not unworthy of you. I shall be very good & send money all the winter – as I am now – I am in good health – free from debts & all cares, my prospects in business brighter than they have yet been – so, dear Addey, if you will only be kind & good like you once were, let your love again take root & strengthen with its growth, & we will be happy. Write to me often & longer letters. Do not fear me – nor my love. If at times it is obscured or dimmed by clouds of perplexity

& trouble, hope will always clear it away & shew it bright and strong as ever.

Good bye and God bless us,
Give my love to all,
George

I like to think these are true love letters, not just the usual ones where high-sounding and frothy sentiments predominate. Theirs convey what is in their hearts, even when it is hard for the other to hear. It appears as if Addey has at least considered breaking their engagement, from what he says in his last letter.

It has been another year of misunderstanding and alienation for them both, and thankfully, one of the last. He makes an almost desperate plea for her to restore her faith in and love for him.

1855

Put your bonnet on & come along, Addey

Though they don't know it, 1855 is to be the last year of their long and difficult courtship. For more than three years they have been separated, with George unable to set aside funds or make a viable plan for her to join him. This fourth year begins on the same note, with George acknowledging his improvidence and still vacillating on whether to return to England to escort her back or for her to come across the ocean alone.

16 January 1855 26 John Street

My dear Addey,

I need scarcely tell you how glad I was to receive your last letter. I am a great deal more to blame than you for what you have said or done to ask forgiveness from me. 'Tis I who should ask your pardon which I now do most penitently. I will promise to be a better boy in future so let us kiss & make friends once more.

For the last two or three months since I gave up the Bleak House, I have not been as careful over my exchequer as I ought to be for I could not prevent myself from entertaining the notion that you no longer cared anything about me and I became careless & stupid, of course – but since I received your letter January 1 I have improved wonderfully & now I will tell you more about what I purpose doing.

By the beginning of May I shall be enabled to come home to England & with your permission get married then & afterwards just have sufficient funds to enable us to return to this country where I shall find a berth open for me worth $800 per annum, not much, certainly, & we shall have to live very quietly, but I think with prudence & care we can manage to get along until better times turn up. You know, my dear Addey, that in consulting only my own selfish feelings on the matter, I should not get married at all until I were my own master, but as this cannot be at present, I will submit to be dependent for some years longer rather than we should be longer separated for I feel quite sure it does neither of us any good to be so long, so very very long away from each other.

It may be that when I return I shall find some inducement offered to remain in England which I would almost rather do. Or it would I believe be more economical in a pecuniary sense for you to come out to me alone – but I seem to have quite an aversion to this idea, & it will not cost such a great deal more for me to come home & fetch you.

What changes have taken place within the last three years & you think I am changed too. Well, it may be so, but I think it is only superficially. At heart I think I am about the same. I wonder if you are changed. I don't know how it is with you, Addey, but I don't seem to feel now as though I were writing to you, but more as unto a stranger. We must see & talk to each other before we shall be quite like the old friends we used to be. Good bye, dear, and give my love to everybody & believe in the constancy & truth of

Ever yours,
Affectionately,
GL Virtue

I used to love you most, I think, when we were alone and our thoughts alike, pure & free from form & conventionality – our souls then did seem to harmonize, & we both felt free & happy in each other's love & confidence. Do you ever have the same thoughts now that you did then, or are you changed – or am I?

3 April 1855 121 Court Street, Boston

My dear Addey,

You will see by the heading of my letter that I have removed from New York. I took possession here last Wednesday.

My line of conduct is now quite plain before me. I only have to make a good business here & it will pay me well. I am sanguine – more so, in fact, than I have been since I left England.

Of course this sudden change will alter my determination of coming home this summer. Now, don't begin to kick up a row about it, because, my dear, it would really cost a lot of money, and I do not see that we should be any better for it in any way. The only advantage would be that I should be enabled to escort you over which is what I have long hoped for, but it is not to be, & therefore it is no use to be forever aiming at what I cannot accomplish. You can as well come over by one of the Boston steamers this summer – & that will end the matter at once.

I am almost ashamed to tell you but as I like you always to know the truth, I will be candid. I have only saved a few pounds, nothing in fact worth speaking of, but I have enough furniture for us to begin housekeeping in a small way & I have a small salary of $800.00 per annum with a commission on the increase of business. Do you think we two can manage with this to start with? Because if you don't, why then we must wait I suppose until I can earn more. Just think it over & tell me what you think is best to be done, only for God's sake, let us think & act more in concert with each other & not be biased so much as I believe we both are by the opinions & thoughts of others. It seems such a long time to me since our souls moved in harmony. I am very much to blame, I know, but this long, dreary, sickening absence has made a great change in both of us, I think – but it should not. Our hearts should still be the same to each other – are they? Write to me a good long letter soon. Address it to me here – & try to have more confidence in me.

Your ever,
G.L.V.

Boarding is rather expensive here but I am at no other expense so that by the end of May with God's blessing I will be prepared to send you over a draft for your passage if you will by that time be ready to come.

Boston you will be much pleased with. I like it infinitely better than New York. It is more like an English city than any place I have been in yet. I think we shall be very jolly here. Hurrah, when I think of seeing you again so soon. My dear, it makes me think of old times & feel there is happiness in store for us yet. Give us a kiss,

Good bye,

I am yet troubled in my mind sometimes as to the best way for your coming out – I mean, alone. The Boston steamer from Liverpool is the correct idea, I believe. But elect your own way, my dear, only don't I wish I could trot over & fetch you, that's all.

George's confidence and resolve have been reignited after a move to Boston. At long last, he decides she must come to him. Never one to hold back, Addey expresses her disappointment at having to cross the ocean alone.

What courage it must have taken for her to venture forth from her home in beautiful Devon, leaving her father, who would now be bereft of family, to come to a new world, to a new life, and to George, whom she truly loves, but who thus far has shown little promise of being able to support them. She has decided her fate, relying on her own strength and good sense to serve her well.

1 May 1855 Peckham Rye

My dearest George,

I have to thank you for your last two letters. They were more like the letters of old and afforded me much pleasure. The cloud that has rested on and somewhat dimmed the brightness of our love and faith is passing away. May never another darken our continual affection. I assure you, dear George, I feel far more happy and contented than I have done for some time. Do you? It is misery to doubt. We have both been unhappy, dearest, but it is past.

I am very, very much disappointed that I shall have to go alone across the ocean. After all, in this one particular, I suppose we *are* to be disappointed, and so it is useless to complain.

I spent the day yesterday in Finsbury Square. They are all glad of your decision, and think it quite right (and I suppose it is). They are anxious that I should go to you as soon as may be.

James suggested, and we all agree, that it would be far better for me to go to New York instead of Boston, for many reasons. If I go to the former place, your aunt says Mrs. Roberts will receive me at her house where I can remain until we are married which you know, dearest, would be far preferable to going to a hotel or boarding house, as I should be obliged to do if I went to Boston. When Mrs. Roberts was in England she promised Mrs. Virtue that she would receive me on my arrival, and would be as kind as if I were her own child, and that I should be married from her house and that I should not leave her until all was "right," all of which is very kind. I feel very much obliged to Mrs. Roberts and your aunt for the interest they take in us.

Then you know you could be at New York to receive me. Be sure you do this for fancy how lonely I should be if you were not there. They say there are so many more persons going to New York than to Boston, that there would be much greater likelihood of my meeting with pleasant people and of their knowing somebody who may be going there.

I think, dear, I had rather go in a sailing vessel than in a steamer. I wish I knew some captain and his wife who are going to make the voyage. However, if not, I am quite able to take care of myself, I flatter myself. And about the time, your uncle thinks if I go in the hot weather, the change of climate would be very likely to make me ill. He would advise my waiting until the intense heat is past, say July. What do you say to all this? Write soon and tell me all about it. I have obeyed your request, and have thought it well over as you bade me. I am quite content to share your fortunes, whatever they may be. I look forward to our marriage as to the commencement of our happiness for we were ever happier together than apart. Yes! George, dearest, we shall be very happy. We must allow no clouds to shadow our married life. We must have no thought concealed from each other. We must be in deed as one. Can we not be all this, dearest? And we shall indeed be happy.

Frances is going to write to Mrs. Roberts today to enquire if they know of anybody who is going to America soon, under whose care I might be placed, and to remind her of her promise. I think you will agree with us that this arrangement will be far more *proper* than my going entirely amongst strangers.

22 MAY 1855

121 COURT STREET
BOSTON

My dear little Addey,

Your letter of the 1st I received yesterday. I am very glad to think we are once more getting good friends again – not that I believe we have ever been anything else in reality – only that we have misunderstood each other. But it's all over now, isn't it? I wish I could just give you a kiss to assure you of my love. Wait till you come over & I'll make up for lost time, and do you think I wouldn't come to New York to meet you on your arrival? Why my dear little soul, I'd walk barefoot twice as far to see you, but when I know you are coming all this distance alone for my sake, why I can only say you are a little trump. I love you always, Addey, but most when you stand out, as it were, alone in the world, trusting only to yourself & to me. 'Tis then I feel my heart grow big and a feeling of strength & peace & happiness makes me almost a different being. When we get married we will have a little quarrel now & then if you like – just for the pleasure of making it up again – or would you rather not?

I am sorry to hear that Uncle George has been unwell & hope the change of air will do him good. About the time of coming over, I agree with him in thinking the fall would be the best time, unless you have made up your mind to come over with Miss Perry. Until I hear from you again, I shall not know how you have decided. It certainly would be better for you to come to New York first, but if you come in a sailing vessel, I shall not know exactly the time you will arrive. However I will make what preparations I can. I shall be glad when we are quietly settled down in our little home. I must look out for a suitable place right away. I have been stopping at a hotel since I have been in Boston, but now I know you are really coming out so soon, I must prepare myself to meet you. Be sure you write soon & let me know if you have decided on coming out with Miss Perry. If you *have not* I think the idea of coming to New York is the best plan.

Love & kisses to all
Geo L. Virtue

I wonder if Tom Glanville could learn what had become of poor Brother John's wife & child. I should like to know how they have been provided for since his death.

20 July 1855

Prospect Villa
Peckham Rye
Surrey

My dearest George,

I have no letter of yours to answer for I have not heard from you since I last wrote, but I have so much to tell you, enough if I were a clever letter writer to fill three or four sheets of paper, but unfortunately I have not the gift of spinning out a few facts into a folio like Annie Glanville.

Well then, dear, to begin, I have been staying nearly a fortnight with your sister. While I was there your father came up to see me and staid from Saturday until Monday. I like him exceedingly. He is so kind, and pleasant, and I believe I have made a favorable impression also for he entirely approves of his son's choice and calls me his "dear little daughter-in-law." I took a walk with him on Primrose Hill on Sunday. Edward joined us on our way and in the afternoon we all took tea at your Uncle James'. Monday morning he left us and on that day also, I took leave of my own dear father. (He is gone back to Totnes.) It was a sad parting as you may imagine, poor old man! And now he must be so lonely, separated, as he says, from all he holds dear on earth. It makes me sad when I think of him. I do so wish Winnie was home. By the way, Winnie has another son. That makes four, you know.

Alicia and myself are now going to call on a lady who is thinking of going to America next month. She is a French woman and intends to sail, so if we can manage to go together, it will make it very pleasant. Your aunt, George, says she is a most energetic woman and will take all trouble off my hands. When we have arranged all about it, I will write again, only, dear George, I wish you would write; it seems such a long time since I had a letter from you, and *now* too, when I am to see you so soon.

You will be surprised when I tell you that we are expecting Spencer home this month, or at the latest, next. We expected when he left that he would return somewhere about next Christmas. It seems almost impossible that he should have made such a long voyage and back in less than six months, and yet he has and staid two months in China. He has arranged his business more satisfactorily than he expected, I believe. I shall be dreadfully disappointed if he does not come back before I leave.

Did you expect this would tell you when I should leave. Patience! I shall know soon, I suppose. It makes me very nervous, I assure you, dearest, when I think of the step we are just on the eve of taking. I shall not enter into the new tie lightly. I feel that I am – that we are both taking a greater responsibility upon ourselves – and I pray that I may make you a good wife. You must bear with me, dearest. You will find that I have lots of faults but I trust to your love and believe we shall both be happy. I think our love and faith in each other have been pretty well tried, and have not been found wanting.

➣ *Amen to that, Addey.*

I am to have a portrait of your father and your young sister, who Mrs. Lawrence says is not the least like you were. Also, I am promised portraits of Harriet, and Edward and Tom if possible, but he is at present out of London.

Ever yours,
Addey

➣ *The above is Addey's last letter to George, sent before her sailing on the ship* Southampton *to New York on August 23rd.*

29 August 1855 121 Court Street, Boston

My dear Addey,

I think I am very impatient for I almost expect a letter from you every mail, but I have not heard from you since August 2nd, not quite a month, although it seems an age.

Of course I feel very anxious to hear about how you have decided on coming out, or are you still unsettled in this respect. I wish it was all settled & you were on the passage out; my mind would then be made up as to what course I should take & I could make my arrangements for meeting you in New York, but in the present unsettled state of affairs I cannot think right at all, so do you make your mind up very soon, my dear, & let me know.

Put your bonnet on & come along, Addey. Never mind the traps; we shall have plenty of time to look after them when we are more settled.

Sometimes I have disagreeable thoughts creeping into my mind, that perhaps you don't want to come; that my apparent coldness & indifference (as my past letters may have led you to conceive) has warped & changed your feelings towards me, & that you no longer think of me as you used to. Many more such thoughts as these are continually intruding themselves on my mind which makes me feel anything but jolly under the circumstances. If there is the slightest foundation for any such unpleasant forebodings as these, I beg you will not hesitate to tell me.

Anyhow, write, Addey. Write if you love me – or write if you don't – only don't keep a fellow in this state of miserable suspense.

I daresay I shall get one of your kind letters next mail (& this I always say to myself) which will quite explain away all these unpleasant thinkings, & then I shall be sorry for letting you see what a fretful, impatient fellow I have become – but I shall let this go now I have written it & trust for better hopes.

G. L. V.

If I don't get a letter next mail, I'll swear & chew tobacco, there!

13 September 1855 121 Court Street

My dearest Addey,

If I could but tell with certainty the day you would arrive, I would be in New York at that time without fail, but as there is no certainty of what time the *Southampton* will arrive I must perforce leave you in the hands of kind friends until I hear of your arrival, when I will immediately come on to New York.

I am going to give this note to Mr. Emmins who is in Boston at present & he promises me he will have it delivered to you the moment the *Southampton* arrives. You do not know, my dear, how much I wish to see you. I am very anxious to hear of your safe arrival too. The westerly winds have prevailed for the last two weeks. I calculate you are about fifteen hundred miles from me just at this present time. I wonder if you are thinking of me.

I hope, my dear, you will not think any the worse of me because I shall not be in New York when you arrive – it is my wish! The business here is of such a nature, it will not admit of my being away for an unlimited period as there is no certainty to a week as to when you may arrive.

I received a kind letter from your father this morning which I shall answer by the next steamer. He consigns his youngest daughter to my care (in all confidence) with your mother's dying request, "Be always kind to Addey under all circumstances."

He may rest assured of it & you have confidence in me or you would never have ventured so far for my sake.

Good bye my son. You will hear me whistle soon.

Ever yours,
G.L.V.

A Sevear Strugell

The following letter to George from Addey's father, Thomas Watson, never fails to stir me. Though his syntax and spelling are eccentric, if endearing (at least to me), he gets his message across. My heart breaks for him.

25 August 1855 Totnes

My Dear George,

If I know you as I believe I do you will appreciate this familiar term as I now consider you my son. My *dearest child* has now been on board the ship *Southampton* the two last nights, and is on her way to *you* and the new world. May God bless her and protect her safely to its shores.

My dear George, I assure you I am *still* in the midst of a very sevear strugell in parting with her as it seems it may be forever and she is my last and very *dear child*. Moreover, she was left to me with these dying words of her dear mother, "Be kind to Addey in all circumstances" but now she is quite out of my power and I must give her up with my most earnest prayers unto him who is mighty to save that she may be carried safe to your shores and to your care and protection. I cannot use more striking words than those that were impressed upon my mind though I trust I needed not to be reminded, nor do I think that you do. Nevertheless, may they have the same effects upon you as they had upon me, and I will say for your own and her happyness and for the sake of a poor old man, as I am sorry to tell you that I am, "You will be *kind* to my dear Addey under all circumstances" and I with the greatest confidence do assure you that she will deserve it.

My dear George, I have been introduced to your father, to your sister & to one of your brothers whom I consider a very amebeall young man, and have also seen the Missies Vertue, your cousins. You will wonder perhaps how I should be such an old man as you left me but a few years since in the prime of life, but I have been nearly three years in very bad health and under the doctors but am now, thank God, quite recovered, but do not think I shall ever get young again as I am now nearly 70, but have lost *all* and have now, as it were, no *wife* and no *children* (near me) and consequently no comforts – and still there is much pleasure in thinking that my children are mostly comfortably situated. I shall look forward with greatest ansciaty to here from my dear Addey as soon as she arrives on the shores of America which I sepose will not be until the end of September.

We have here a very late harvest. The farmers are now very busy cutting what little there is, the corn not so fine as last year, the potatoes very bad, apples scarce & breadstuff very dear. All are complaining about the procrastination of the war.

Well, my dear George, may it please God to bless you both, my dear children, and may you live very *happy* together. You will be in the constant prayer of your

Affectionate father,
T. Watson

Postmarked 27 August 1855 from Totnes – arrives 11 September
Addressed to Mr. George Vertue, 121 Court Street, Boston, America

He expresses his sadness at saying goodbye to his youngest daughter, knowing there is little likelihood of his ever seeing her again. He has given her the greatest parental gift, the freedom to pursue her own destiny. I wonder how he spent the rest of his days. I trust he had a chance now and then to shoot a brace of partridge.

On September 19, 1855, Addey arrived in New York on the sailing ship Southampton. *George received news of her coming and went to New York to meet her. All the travails of their long time apart must have fallen away as the two of them saw one another again after nearly five years of separation. What a joyous reunion it must have been.*

George returned to Boston until the wedding was to take place, while Addey stayed with the Roberts in Brooklyn. George wrote the three following letters from 121 Court Street in his inimitable buoyant style. In one of them he mentions that he has allowed an hour for a quiet chat before the ceremony. Perhaps Addey was jittery, as most brides are, but also she was in an unfamiliar place and had no one from her family with her. She must have welcomed a few quiet moments with him before the ceremony, a time to share their thoughts on the step they were about to take.

27 September 1855 121 Court Street, Boston

My dear Addey,

I arrived in Boston well & hearty about 7 o'clock this morning.

I am not quite sure sometimes whether or no it isn't all a dream – but to relieve my mind from all sorts of doubts on the matter, just write to me & tell me all about what you do & where you go & what you think & all that you know. The fact is I am very busy this afternoon making up for (gained) time so you will please to excuse haste.

When you go out, look out for the open cellar doors & uneven pavements & the ferry slips and all that.

I feel almost sorry I did not inveigle you on board the Boston boat by mistake.

"Sebastopol is taken" & Joe won my bottle of champagne – hurrah for the Allies.

Yours ever & ever,
GL Virtue

Kind regards to all @ Willoughby Street including Charlie

A few days later, the next one follows with an insouciant lack of concern about the form of the ceremony, which is so like George. The Virtue wit has endured to the present.

3 OCTOBER 1855 121 COURT STREET, BOSTON

My dear Addey,

I don't care much about the form of marriage, providing, of course, that it be all done legally! But as we had as I thought determined on going to church I do not see that it is worthwhile to alter that arrangement. One coach will hold four of us & take us snugly to the church & bring us back, man & wife, i.e. you & I, I mean, unless Miss Ridgeway & Mr. Pabst catch the infection. We shall have to have a coach anyway, so it may as well be an hour earlier.

If you are not ready by Tuesday, Addey, I'm afraid I shall not leave here until Monday evening.

Of course I love you, my dear, but how can a fellow talk about love when he is up to his eyes in books, & rows with men, & all that. You have all my heart – & I feel very proud that you still love me.

Good bye, Dolly Varden,
Ever yours,
G.L.V.

Put only in your trunk just those things you will require for three or four days. The other three boxes I will mail up when I come down & send to Boston by express.

➢ *Dolly Varden is described as "a bright, fresh, conquettish girl, the very personification of good humor and blooming beauty" in Pierce's* Dickens Dictionary.

➢ *This letter is George's last before their wedding:*

6 October 1855 121 Court Street, Boston

My dearest Addey,

I received your kind letter this morning, also one from Brother Pabst, in which he informs me that he had spoken with the Reverend Paddock of St. Peter's Church @ Hoyt & Bond Streets, Brooklyn. The kind gentleman will be ready for us at his church on Tuesday morning. Reverend Paddock is son-in-law to Mr. Jones who came out in the *Southampton.*

D. V. [*deo volente*, God willing], I shall leave here Saturday afternoon – shall put up @ Mrs. Gerard's where I shall breakfast & call @ Mr. Roberts early (say 9 o'clock) in time for a quiet chat before church time. Hope the weather will be fine. I'm glad you have fixed on Tuesday. The cards are done, intended to have sent you one, but left them home this morning. Won't forget to put them in my carpet bag. Madame Hill is a French lady & a very nice amiable little person. You will be more comfortable there than @ Dame Carlyle's. Don't be nervous, my dear – it's all right at last & we shall be very happy. I feel very thankful that we are to be united after such a long parting. Good bye,

Yours ever,
George

On Tuesday morning, October 9, 1855, at Saint Peter's Episcopal Church in Brooklyn, New York, George Virtue and Adelaide Watson became man and wife, married by the rector, the Reverend John Paddock. It was the happy ending they had long sought, and the beginning of their married life together.

And as the curtain rose for the two of you on your married life, it fell sadly and irrevocably on your sharing with me your distinctive and singularly engaging personalities, your fondest and most troubling thoughts, and a world long since vanished. Your presence has been a rare gift, which has enhanced my life and strengthened immeasurably my appreciation of and love for our family.

I am proud and pleased to be your descendant.

Epilogue

And then:

After the wedding, George and Addey returned to Boston, where George worked for Virtue & Company at 121 Court Street. They lived in Waverly, a small town outside the city. A son, George Francis (Frank), was born on September 8, 1856, just a year after they wed. A second son, Lawrence, was born in November 1857. He lived only three months. On July 3rd, 1859, Herbert Spencer Virtue was born, and years later became the grandfather I knew and loved. They also had three daughters, Bessie, Harriet Louisa (Aunt Louie), and Mabel, and another son, Arthur, who carried on the business after his father's death.

In 1861, George was summoned back to the New York office, working there until 1867, when the family moved to Toronto. George and Addey lived out the rest of their lives there. He is listed in the Toronto archives as a publisher and printer during the 1870s and '80s.

It is no surprise he was a good husband and a kind father. Addey's faith in him was fulfilled. With the help of her strong moral sense and predilection for keeping him on the straight and narrow (and his appreciation of her for doing so), plus his own many fine qualities, he became a responsible and upstanding citizen, providing well for his large family. He was a member and at one time the president of the St. George's Society, the preeminent philanthropic organization of Toronto.

They lived together for 39 years until his death in March 1894. Addey lived for another twenty years, until 1914. They are buried together in the Mount Pleasant cemetery in Toronto beneath an imposing stone of pink granite resembling a giant chess piece, where Addey

has joined George in what I hope was their final reunion. Their daughter Bessie and Addey's sister Alicia are also there. The woman at the office of the cemetery told me there was room in the family plot for more Virtues if any should want it to be their final resting place.

Digging through old documents and archives can in no way match the spell cast by the inimitable voices of Addey and George. Their warmth and spirit are present in the eloquence of their words. They have become a part of my inner world as I have been granted access to a small part of theirs. Most of what we do in life vanishes, slipping through the cracks of memory without a trace into the oblivion of time, that silent, inexorable predator. These letters capture and preserve a small sliver of their humanity, a window through which to peer, providing a glimmer of immortality: that they were here and mattered. Each of us arrives on this earth – and then departs again after a short stay, as part of an eternal and unfathomable mystery.

Their story is a truly romantic one, told by them with skill, candor, and grace with an edge of intimacy all their own. Perhaps their words will continue to touch future generations, with their tale of love, struggle, and triumph – of *Virtue Rewarded.*

Virtue & Yorston, Toronto

Obituary of George Virtue

The death is announced of Mr. George Virtue, an old and highly-respected resident of Toronto who passed away on Saturday at his residence, 11 Isabella Street. Mr. Virtue had suffered from an illness about two years ago, but he had recovered sufficiently to continue at his business. Shortly before Christmas, however, he was taken ill again, and it soon became evident that he could not recover. He was a native of England, and came to New York when a young man. After spending some time in the employ of a metropolitan publishing house, he went into business as a publisher in that city on his own account. Twenty-six years ago he came to Toronto and established the well-known publishing business which is still in existence and which is now being carried on by his son, Arthur G. Virtue. The late Mr. Virtue was a prominent member of St. George's Society, and was elected to the presidency of that organization in 1882. For ten years he was one of its most active stewards and in that capacity took on its benevolent work. He was a member of the Bond Street Congregational Church and was for many years a steward in politics. Mr. Virtue was a liberal, but he never identified himself prominently with the warfare of the parties. He leaves behind him a widow, three sons and three daughters. Mr. Virtue was a generous, kindhearted and lovable man.

Died March 3, 1894

The Watsons

Addey is the youngest of the five Watson children. Her elder brother Thomas is never mentioned in the letters. In the Galton papers, he is described as having succumbed to drink. His wife left him, taking their six children. It is also noted that he eventually pulled himself together and lived quietly somewhere in the country.

William, the second son, lives in Cockfosters in North London with his wife and children. He operates a nursery business there, raising ten children, no small feat. George visits him occasionally when he is working in London, speaking of his visits with pleasure.

There are three Watson daughters:

The eldest, Alicia, is engaged to Spencer Compton, who is involved with the East India trade. He is either on the high seas or in Asia for extended periods of time. They are engaged for thirteen years before they marry.

Winnie, the middle daughter, emigrates to India in August of 1849 to marry Tom Glanville, who is a Wesleyan missionary there. He later gave up this work because preaching gave him "bilious headaches." Winnie and Tom had eleven children. His sister Annie is a friend of Addey's. She is mentioned frequently in the letters. Annie's brother Jem is a friend of George's.

The three sisters were close, as is clear in the letters. I was surprised, however, to discover that Alicia is buried with George and Addey in the Mount Pleasant Cemetery in Toronto. She was in Toronto when Herbert went to England in 1878.

Some additional information about the Watson family was provided by a questionnaire that Winnie filled out for Francis Galton's *A Record of Family Faculties,* a study of the inheritance of family traits. Winnie gave her own slant to her assessment of her relatives' strengths and weaknesses.

The Virtues

George grew up in Bristol, where his father, Francis, was a bookseller.

There were six Virtue brothers and one sister. The oldest was John, next Harriet, with a brother William also born in 1826, which may indicate that they were twins. George is the middle child, third son, fourth child, born in 1828. Three younger brothers, James, Edward, and Thomas, are mentioned in the letters, with George often remarking that they have not distinguished themselves. He hopes to do better, though he speaks fondly of them.

George's sister Harriet is married to a man named Lawrence. George lives with Harriet and her family in Camden Town when he starts working for Virtue & Company in London.

Time present and time past
Are both perhaps present in time future,
And time future contained in time past.

T. S. Eliot, "Burnt Norton"

Acknowledgments

Michael Virtue, my cousin, gave me much help and information. He was the last head of Virtue & Company, Ltd. His father, **Guy Virtue**, was my introduction to the English contingent of Virtues.

Tony Fillingham, Mary's son, filled me in on the visits of Aunt Louie to his household when he was a small boy. He remembered her fondly as being very pretty, and lots of fun.

Another descendant, **Judy Schneider**, I found on the internet. As a relative, she shares my interest in the Virtues. She has added archival and personal information and become a good friend as well.

My sister, **Joyce Stevens**, retrieved and transcribed the letters. She is the family archivist, and has given me research material and the benefit of her extensive knowledge.

The photo of the letters on the cover was taken by professional photographer **Lee Nadel**.

Steve Harris was my computer guru, who shepherded me through the challenges of working on three different computers.

I thank **David Teele**, who has skillfully worked on the old photos and has offered valuable advice.

I am indebted to Toronto friends **Marilyn Short and Jeff Weiss**, with whom I stayed while doing research there. They ferried me about, wined and dined me, and were taken aback, as was I, when we discovered that their office was at the corner of George and Adelaide Streets.

My writing group, **Glo Masterson**, **Catherine McGeary**, **Mary Cole**, and **Yhanna Coffin**, have been invaluable, individually and as a group, in their long and sustained dedication, their feedback, and particularly their unstinting belief that I would complete this project.

Finally, I am grateful for the talented efforts of my editor and "book maker," **Ruth Maassen,** whose technical skills and judgment have resulted in bringing the story of Addey and George's courtship into the twenty-first century, where it – and they – can be known by present and future generations.